Leveled Readers Assessment

Primary
Grades K-3

Harcourt School P[...]

www.harcourtschool.com

Copyright © by Harcourt, Inc.

All rights reserved. No part of this publication may be reproduced or transmitted in any form or by any means, electronic or mechanical, including photocopy, recording, or any information storage and retrieval system, without permission in writing from the publisher.

Permission is hereby granted to individuals using the corresponding student's textbook or kit as the major vehicle for regular classroom instruction to photocopy Copying Masters from this publication in classroom quantities for instructional use and not for resale. Requests for information on other matters regarding duplication of this work should be addressed to School Permissions and Copyrights, Harcourt, Inc., 6277 Sea Harbor Drive, Orlando, Florida 32887-6777. Fax: 407-345-2418.

The Chart of Levels is intended to help teachers in purchasing leveled books from Harcourt. Please note the following:

(1) Reading Recovery® is a registered service mark of The Ohio State University.
(2) The complete Reading Recovery® book list, created by the Reading Recovery® Council of North America, includes books from numerous publishers since a premise of the program is that children be provided with a range of texts. One publisher's book list alone is not suffcent to implement a Reading Recovery® program.
(3) Levels are subject to change as they are periodically tested and reevaluated.

STORYTOWN is a trademark of Harcourt, Inc. HARCOURT and the Harcourt Logo are trademarks of Harcourt, Inc., registered in the United States of America and/or other jurisdictions.

Printed in China

ISBN 10: 0-15-358789-X   ISBN 13: 978-0-15-358789-4

4 5 6 7 8 9 10 0940 16 15 14 13 12 11 10 09

If you have received these materials as examination copies free of charge, Harcourt School Publishers retains title to the materials and they may not be resold. Resale of examination copies is strictly prohibited and is illegal.

Possession of this publication in print format does not entitle users to convert this publication, or any portion of it, into electronic format.

Table of Contents

Individual Reading Inventories

Introduction

Using the Leveled Readers for Assessment

Matching children with books requires teachers to make judgments about the children themselves—their backgrounds, interests, and reading skills. To help with this task, a group of Leveled Readers have been selected to serve as benchmark books to help teachers assess children's reading levels. For each level—Below-Level, On-Level, and Advanced—three Leveled Readers have been identified to help match children to texts with which they will be successful. These benchmark books, along with the appropriate assessment data, will help determine what children are capable of reading, what they are ready to learn, and how to group them most effectively for instruction. (For English learners, group children according to academic levels and assign Leveled Readers as appropriate.)

Leveling books is not an exact science, and several criteria must be taken into account. In general, the reading levels in this book were developed based on the work of Irene C. Fountas and Gay Su Pinnell as outlined in titles such as *Guided Reading: Good First Teaching for All Children* (Heinemann, 1996), *Guiding Readers and Writers (Grades 3–6): Teaching Comprehension, Genre, and Content Literacy,* (Heinemann, 2001), and *Leveled Books for Readers, Grades 3-6: A Companion Volume to Guiding Readers and Writers* (Heinemann, 2001).

Passages from the Leveled Readers can be used for evaluation at three different points during the school year. (See page 7 for a chart of these evaluation points.) For each passage, two assessment instruments are provided:

- The Individual Reading Inventory (IRI) Summary Form on page 44 is a generic form that should be copied and re-used for each book.

- The IRI pages themselves, pages 45–122, provide specific information for each book, including a summary and five comprehension questions.

It is important to use a Leveled Reader as an assessment tool *before* you use it for instruction. That way, the child will not be already familiar with the text. The book can be presented by reading its introduction and by having the child read the title and make predictions about what he or she will read. Then the child reads the passage aloud. His or her miscues are recorded on the Individual Reading Inventory Summary Form. A *Comments* section is provided for making notes about the child's use of strategies and his or her attitude toward reading. Literal and inferential questions are provided to assess comprehension. If the passage is at the child's instructional level, he or she will score with 90–95 percent accuracy on the Error Rate and the Fluency Rate, and with 80 percent accuracy on Comprehension. A child scoring at these rates has "met the benchmark."

Some teachers prefer to use retellings instead of, or in addition to, questions to assess comprehension. Rubrics for performing retelling evaluations for fiction and nonfiction are provided on pages 35–36. If both a retelling and questions are used, the child should retell the story first. Any questions not answered in the retelling can then be asked. Teachers should use their professional judgment to decide whether the child's comprehension is at an accuracy level of 80 percent.

If the child meets the benchmark, he or she is ready for instruction at that level. If the child has too many errors, or reads the book with almost perfect accuracy, reassess either lower or higher to find the child's instructional level.

Children at approximately the same level can be assigned to guided reading groups. Within these groups, the teacher can support children's use of strategies by modeling the things that good readers do, such as thinking about whether a word makes sense, self-correcting, and rereading. At the next evaluation point, the child can be assessed at a higher level. Gradually, children will progress, level by level, toward becoming fluent, lifelong readers.

Evaluation Points Chart

The following chart includes dates based on a typical school year. You may need to adjust these dates to your particular school's calendar.

	October (Theme 2)	February (Theme 4)	May (Theme 6)
Grade K	**OL:** *Come in the Barn,* GR: B **AL:** *I Like What I See,* GR: C	**OL:** *We Want a Pet,* GR: C **AL:** *The Pet for Us,* GR: D	**BL:** *Letters and Sounds, Review 2,* GR: B **OL:** *Pam and Hal,* GR: C **AL:** *Ben Has to Go!* GR: E
Grade 1	**BL:** *Use Your Feet!,* GR: E **OL:** *Cliff's Feet,* GR: E **AL:** *Home Run,* GR: F	**BL:** *In the Desert,* GR: F **OL:** *In the Snow,* GR: H **AL:** *In the Tropics,* GR: I	**BL:** *Hedgehog and Beaver Have a Picnic,* GR: I **OL:** *Duck's Visit,* GR: J **AL:** *Raccoon and Otter Make Muffins,* GR: K
Grade 2	**BL:** *Apples for Sheep and Goat,* GR: H **OL:** *The Country Show,* GR: J **AL:** *Rooster's Sore Throat,* GR: M	**BL:** *Thomas Alva Edison: A Great Inventor,* GR: K **OL:** *Madam C.J. Walker: Making Dreams Happen,* GR: L **AL:** *Cyrus McCormick: Friend to Farmers,* GR: N	**BL:** *Abalone and the Sea,* GR: K **OL:** *How the Tortoise Got Its Shell,* GR: M **AL:** *Why Tree Frog Sings at Night,* GR: O
Grade 3	**BL:** *How Bear Lost His Tail,* GR: M **OL:** *The Coat of Patches, A Yiddish Folktale,* GR: O **AL:** *The Stonecutter,* GR: P	**BL:** *Favorite Fables,* GR: N **OL:** *Coyote and Rabbit, A Tale from the Southwest,* GR: P **AL:** *Groundhog's New Home,* GR: Q	**BL:** *Earth's Moon,* GR: O **OL:** *Star Patterns in the Sky,* GR: P **AL:** *The Sun and the Stars,* GR: R

NOTE: Guided Reading (GR) levels are based upon the work of Fountas and Pinnell as well as other criteria to allow for a different reading level for any given child. These criteria include a child's personal interest, background knowledge, and language skills.

Characteristics of Text

Books at the following Guided Reading levels tend to exhibit these characteristics:

Level A	• consistent placement of print, with separation between print and pictures
	• one line of text per page
	• ample space separating words
	• repeated words and sentence structures
	• highly familiar words and concepts
	• illustrations that are very supportive of text
	• single idea or simple story line
Levels B–C	• consistent placement of print, with separation between print and pictures
	• may present more than one line of text per page
	• ample space separating words
	• repeated words and sentence structures
	• familiar words and concepts
	• illustrations that are very supportive of text
	• single idea or simple story line
Levels D–G	• amount of text is gradually increasing
	• varied sentence patterns
	• slightly more difficult vocabulary, including words with inflected endings
	• illustrations support reading but text carries more meaning
	• dialogue may appear
	• punctuation supports phrasing and meaning
	• literary language may be used
	• more complex story structure

Levels H–K	• texts are longer with more sentences per page; chapter books may be included • varied and more complex sentence patterns; literary language • stories may be chronological, with several episodes • descriptions may be extended • some new information may be presented, as in hybrid fiction-nonfiction texts • may develop memorable characters • illustrations provide low to moderate support • vocabulary requires skill in word analysis
Levels L–O	• may include longer books that cannot be read in one sitting • may use smaller print, with less space between words • more text per page • sophisticated vocabulary that may require problem-solving to decode • include a wider variety of genres • complex language structures • less familiar topics, settings, and concepts • characters often learn and change in the course of the story
Levels P to End-Year Grade 5	• Characteristics are similar to levels L–O, except: • Scores attained by standard readability formulae (Spache for grades K–2; Dale-Chall for grades 3–6) may range from 3.5 to 6.0. • Books that have relatively high readability scores for their grades may be placed at lower levels if they have some of these characteristics: familiar ideas, characters, plots, and settings; natural language structures; little new information; some illustration/graphic support; topics and characters that will interest most readers; little technical or specialized vocabulary; and familiar story conventions. • Books with lower readability scores for the grade may be placed at higher levels if they contain some of these characteristics: unfamiliar ideas, characters, plots, and settings; difficult language structures; much new information; unstated main ideas; abstract ideas and vocabulary; complex relationships among ideas; unusual perspectives; and little or no illustration/graphic support.

© Harcourt

Chart of Levels

Grade	Level: Below–, On–, Advanced, ELL	Title	Reading Recovery®	Guided Reading	DRA
K	BL	Letters and Sounds Mm, Ss	1	A	1
K	BL	Letters and Sounds Rr	1	A	1
K	BL	Letters and Sounds Tt	1	A	1
K	BL	Letters and Sounds Nn, Pp	1	A	1
K	BL	Letters and Sounds Cc	1	A	1
K	BL	Letters and Sounds Aa	1	A	1
K	BL	Letters and Sounds -am, -at, -ap	1	A	1
K	BL	Letters and Sounds Dd	1	A	1
K	BL	Letters and Sounds -ap, -an	1	A	1
K	BL	Letters and Sounds Ii	1	A	1
K	BL	Letters and Sounds Gg, Ff	1	A	1
K	BL	Letters and Sounds -it, -ip, -in	1	A	1
K	BL	Letters and Sounds Bb, Kk	1	A	1
K	BL	Letters and Sounds -in, -ig, -it	1	A	1
K	BL	Letters and Sounds Oo	1	A	1
K	BL	Letters and Sounds Ll, Hh	1	A	1
K	BL	Letters and Sounds -ot, -op	1	A	1
K	BL	Letters and Sounds Ww, Xx	1	A	1
K	BL	Letters and Sounds -ox, -ix, -ax	1	A	1
K	BL	Letters and Sounds Ee	1	A	1

Grade	Level: Below–, On–, Advanced, ELL	Title	Reading Recovery®	Guided Reading	DRA
K	BL	Letters and Sounds -ed, -en	1	A	1
K	BL	Letters and Sounds Vv, Jj	1	A	1
K	BL	Letters and Sounds -et, -eg, -en	1	A	1
K	BL	Letters and Sounds Yy, Zz	1	A	1
K	BL	Letters and Sounds Uu	1	A	1
K	BL	Letters and Sounds -un, -ut, -up	1	A	1
K	BL	Letters and Sounds Qq	1	A	1
K	BL	Letters and Sounds -ug, -up	1	A	1
K	BL	Letters and Sounds, Review 1	2	B	2
K	BL	Letters and Sounds, Review 2	2	B	2
1	BL	Let's Go!	2	B	2
1	BL	Where Are You, Max?	3	C	3
1	BL	Dad Can Tap!	3	C	3
1	BL	Look Out, Mack!	4	C	3
1	BL	Tom and Jill	5	D	4
1	BL	My Home Map	7	E	6
1	BL	Fox Gets Help	7	E	6
1	BL	Jim's Job	7	E	6
1	BL	Dogs Can't Kick	7	E	6
1	BL	Use Your Feet!	7	E	6
1	BL	The Pond	7	E	6
1	BL	The Gold Eggs	7	E	6
1	BL	From Chick to Hen	7	E	6

Grade	Level: Below–, On–, Advanced, ELL	Title	Reading Recovery®	Guided Reading	DRA
1	BL	Carl Can Run	7	E	8
1	BL	Susan L. Roth	9	F	10
1	BL	Room for a Friend	9	F	10
1	BL	The Animal Painter	9	F	10
1	BL	Muffin Surprise	9	F	10
1	BL	Duck Starts a Story	10	F	10
1	BL	In the Desert	10	F	10
1	BL	Kate's Missing Frog	10	F	10
1	BL	We're Going to Make a Hut	10	F	10
1	BL	On the Street	12	G	12
1	BL	The Mystery of the Green Apples	12	G	12
1	BL	Let's Look at Animals	12	G	12
1	BL	Dog Goes to the Sea	12	G	12
1	BL	The Family and the Baby Whale	12	G	12
1	BL	I Am a Pot	14	H	14
1	BL	The Great House	16	I	16
1	BL	Hedgehog and Beaver Have a Picnic	16	I	16
2	BL	Better Than AJ	13	H	14
2	BL	A Surprise for Squirrel and Rabbit	13	H	14
2	BL	Ben and Sooty	13	H	14
2	BL	Cats	13	H	14
2	BL	News from the Market	13	H	14
2	BL	Nancy Lopez – Super Golfer	13	H	14

© Harcourt

Grade	Level: Below–, On–, Advanced, ELL	Title	Reading Recovery®	Guided Reading	DRA
2	BL	Grandma's Rain Song	13	H	14
2	BL	Why Raven Is Black	13	H	14
2	BL	Apples for Sheep and Goat	13	H	14
2	BL	At the Police Station	13	H	14
2	BL	Lucia's Gift	15	I	16
2	BL	Having Fun: Long Ago and Today	15	I	16
2	BL	The Hamster Escape	15	I	16
2	BL	Mountain Babies	15	I	16
2	BL	A Going Away Present	18	J	18–20
2	BL	A New Painting	20	K	18–20
2	BL	Hannah's Dance	18	J	18–20
2	BL	Music Is About Sounds	18	J	18–20
2	BL	Thomas Alva Edison: A Great Inventor	20	K	18–20
2	BL	What's My Pet?	20	K	18–20
2	BL	The Book Sale	20	K	18–20
2	BL	No More Fish!	20	K	18–20
2	BL	The Penguin	20	K	18–20
2	BL	Mountain Gorillas	20	K	18–20
2	BL	At the Library	20	K	18–20
2	BL	Just Like the Moon	20	K	18–20
2	BL	A Writer Named Jean	20	K	18–20
2	BL	Let's Look at Gems	20	K	18–20
2	BL	Abalone and the Sea	20	K	18–20
2	BL	Family Trip	20	K	18–20
3	BL	Lia Leads	20	L	24–28

Grade	Level: Below–, On–, Advanced, ELL	Title	Reading Recovery®	Guided Reading	DRA
3	BL	The Hero	20	L	24–28
3	BL	School Long Ago	20	L	24–28
3	BL	Julia Morgan: Castle Builder	20	L	24–28
3	BL	News Today!	20	M	24–28
3	BL	Nuna Gets a Chance	20	M	24–28
3	BL	Pigeons: Birds Bringing Words	20	M	24–28
3	BL	Talking Senses	20	M	24–28
3	BL	How Bear Lost His Tail	20	M	24–28
3	BL	The Case of the Missing Glass Slipper	20	M	24–28
3	BL	Felix's Turn	20	M	24–28
3	BL	Andrew's Boring Life	20	M	24–28
3	BL	Daffodil Spring	20	M	24–28
3	BL	One Hickory Tree in a Forest	20	M	24–28
3	BL	Ask *Pet Friends!*	20	M	24–28
3	BL	Mano and the Children	20	N	30
3	BL	The Boy and the Bears – A Native American Pawnee Tale	20	N	30
3	BL	Uncle Henry's New Orleans	20	N	30
3	BL	Favorite Fables	20	N	30
3	BL	Listening in on the Orchestra	20	N	30
3	BL	The Everglades	20	N	30
3	BL	Song of the Cicada	20	N	30

Grade	Level: Below–, On–, Advanced, ELL	Title	Reading Recovery®	Guided Reading	DRA
3	BL	Fearless Freddy	20	N	30
3	BL	The Cursive Crisis	20	N	30
3	BL	Cooking with Zork	22	O	34–38
3	BL	The Musical Barn	22	O	34–38
3	BL	Caterpillars and their Cocoons	22	O	34–38
3	BL	Bettina and the Talent Show	22	O	34–38
3	BL	Earth's Moon	22	O	34–38
3	BL	Heart Wise	22	O	34–38
K	OL	Get Ready	1	A	1
K	OL	A Kitchen	1	A	1
K	OL	My Body	1	A	1
K	OL	The Party	1	A	1
K	OL	The City	2	B	2
K	OL	I Can Nap	2	B	2
K	OL	The Bus	2	B	2
K	OL	I Like School	2	B	2
K	OL	Sam Can	2	B	2
K	OL	Come in the Barn	2	B	2
K	OL	This Pig	2	B	2
K	OL	The Pit	3	C	3
K	OL	It Is for Kip	3	C	3
K	OL	Where Do I Go?	2	B	2
K	OL	You Can Go, Ron	3	C	3
K	OL	Where Is My Hat?	3	C	3
K	OL	One, Two, Pop, Pop, Pop!	3	C	3

Grade	Level: Below-, On-, Advanced, ELL	Title	Reading Recovery®	Guided Reading	DRA
K	OL	Go, Max, Go!	3	C	3
K	OL	The Box	3	C	3
K	OL	We Want a Pet	3	C	3
K	OL	Get the Hen!	3	C	3
K	OL	Where Will They Go?	3	C	3
K	OL	They Do a Good Job	4	C	3
K	OL	Will Zig Get Well?	4	C	3
K	OL	In the Tub	4	C	3
K	OL	The Big Bun	4	C	3
K	OL	What Do I Have?	4	C	3
K	OL	Pup on the Go	4	C	3
K	OL	Tim Will Go	3	C	3
K	OL	To the Top	4	C	3
1	OL	Let's Help!	3	C	3
1	OL	In the Van	5	D	3
1	OL	Jill Can Dig	7	E	4
1	OL	Mack Can Tap!	7	E	4
1	OL	Jack and Mom	7	E	4
1	OL	The Pond Map	7	E	6
1	OL	Who Will Help?	7	E	6
1	OL	Liz Can Mix	7	E	6
1	OL	A Puppy Can't Clap	8	E	8
1	OL	Cliff's Feet	8	E	8
1	OL	Hidden in the Forest	8	E	8
1	OL	The Bag of Gold	9	F	10
1	OL	A Kitten Grows	9	F	10

Grade	Level: Below-, On-, Advanced, ELL	Title	Reading Recovery®	Guided Reading	DRA
1	OL	A Card for Mark	10	F	10
1	OL	Amy Hest	11	G	12
1	OL	Always Room for More	11	G	12
1	OL	Can Animals Paint?	12	G	12
1	OL	Sand Surprise	12	G	12
1	OL	An Insect Tale	13	H	14
1	OL	In the Snow	13	H	14
1	OL	Jake Runs Away	14	H	14
1	OL	Let's Play Ball	14	H	14
1	OL	On the Way to the Park	15	I	16
1	OL	The Mystery of the Missing Cat	15	I	16
1	OL	Animals of the Forest	16	I	16
1	OL	Little Pup Goes Down the Road	16	I	16
1	OL	Edmund and Drum and the Baby Turtles	18	J	18
1	OL	Apple Pie	18	J	18
1	OL	The Camping Trip	18	J	18
1	OL	Duck's Visit	18	J	18
2	OL	The Vegetable Garden	15	I	16
2	OL	Bump!	15	I	16
2	OL	Lucy and Billy	15	I	16
2	OL	Ponies	15	I	16
2	OL	Morning News from the Fair	15	I	16
2	OL	Michael Jordan – No Quitter	18	J	18–20
2	OL	Swimming with Pops	18	J	18–20

Grade	Level: Below–, On–, Advanced, ELL	Title	Reading Recovery®	Guided Reading	DRA
2	OL	Hummingbird and Heron	18	J	18–20
2	OL	The Country Show	18	J	18–20
2	OL	Ski Patrol	18	J	18–20
2	OL	Measuring Max	18	J	18–20
2	OL	Riding Bicycles: Long Ago and Today	20	K	18–20
2	OL	The Rabbit Suit Rescue	20	K	18–20
2	OL	Desert Babies	20	K	18–20
2	OL	A Surprise for Mom	20	K	18–20
2	OL	The Best Birthday	20	L	24–28
2	OL	Joshua and the Tigers	20	L	24–28
2	OL	Playing in an Orchestra	20	L	24–28
2	OL	Madame C.J. Walker: Making Dreams Happen	20	L	24–28
2	OL	What's My Sport?	20	L	24–28
2	OL	Jackson's Tree	20	L	24–28
2	OL	Monkey Business	20	L	24–28
2	OL	The Ant	20	M	24–28
2	OL	Orangutans	20	M	24–28
2	OL	A Chat with the Principal	20	M	24–28
2	OL	Wishing for Star Fruit	20	M	24–28
2	OL	Who Is Dr. Seuss?	20	M	24–28
2	OL	Let's Discover Gold	20	M	24–28
2	OL	How the Tortoise Got Its Shell	20	M	24–28
2	OL	An Interesting Trip	20	M	24–28
3	OL	Trust Rey	20	N	30

Grade	Level: Below–, On–, Advanced, ELL	Title	Reading Recovery®	Guided Reading	DRA
3	OL	Music to My Ears	20	N	30
3	OL	A School in a Garden	20	N	30
3	OL	Mary Anning, Fossil Hunter	20	N	30
3	OL	Special Report: The Kicker Cup	20	N	30
3	OL	The Great Race	20	N	30
3	OL	Monkeys: Making a Difference	20	N	30
3	OL	How Do You Say Hello?	20	N	30
3	OL	The Coat of Patches	20	N	30
3	OL	Sherry Holmes and the Case of the Missing Necklace	20	N	30
3	OL	The Battle for Aunt Jane	20	N	30
3	OL	An Ocean Away	20	N	30
3	OL	Wind in the Pines	20	N	30
3	OL	The Life Story of a Barn	20	N	30
3	OL	Special Issue – Brothers and Sisters!	20	N	30
3	OL	A Polar Bear Tale	22	O	34–38
3	OL	How Platypus Came to Be	22	O	34–38
3	OL	Aunt Morgan and Her Murals	22	O	34–38
3	OL	Coyote and Rabbit – A Tale from the Southwest	22	O	34–38
3	OL	Lights! Camera! Action!	22	O	34–38
3	OL	Desert Lives	22	O	34–38
3	OL	Flight of the Monarch	22	O	34–38

Grade	Level: Below–, On–, Advanced, ELL	Title	Reading Recovery®	Guided Reading	DRA
3	OL	Arthur's Summer	22	O	34–38
3	OL	Where the River Begins	22	O	34–38
3	OL	Family 3000	22	O	34–38
3	OL	Oh, to Spin a Web!	22	P	34–38
3	OL	Busy Beaver	22	P	34–38
3	OL	Darlene and the Art Show	22	P	34–38
3	OL	Star Patterns in the Sky	22	P	34–38
3	OL	In the Land of Dinosaurs	22	P	34–38
K	AL	I Sit	2	B	2
K	AL	Jen	2	B	2
K	AL	My Fan	3	C	3
K	AL	I Help	3	C	3
K	AL	Where Is Cam?	3	C	3
K	AL	To the Top	3	C	3
K	AL	The Mat	3	C	3
K	AL	I Like to Go Out	3	C	3
K	AL	See What He Can Do	3	C	3
K	AL	I Like What I See	3	C	3
K	AL	The Fox	4	C	3
K	AL	A Bit for Pip	5	D	4
K	AL	Fun in the Snow	5	D	4
K	AL	Where Can We Go?	4	C	3
K	AL	The Fog	5	D	4
K	AL	Where Did They Go?	5	D	4
K	AL	I Want to Win One	5	D	4
K	AL	Fun for Six	5	D	4
K	AL	Down the Hill	5	D	4

Grade	Level: Below–, On–, Advanced, ELL	Title	Reading Recovery®	Guided Reading	DRA
K	AL	The Pet for Us	5	D	4
K	AL	The Box	5	D	4
K	AL	A Big Job	5	D	4
K	AL	What Is This Job?	5	D	4
K	AL	Zim and Zan	7	E	6
K	AL	The Animal Quiz	7	E	6
K	AL	The Little Egg	7	E	6
K	AL	What a Race!	7	E	6
K	AL	The Party	7	E	6
K	AL	The Map	7	E	6
K	AL	Ben Has to Go!	7	E	6
1	AL	A Hat for Pat	7	E	6
1	AL	The Bag	7	E	6
1	AL	The Milk Van	7	E	8
1	AL	The Backpack	8	E	8
1	AL	Ron and Kim	8	E	8
1	AL	The Store Map	9	F	10
1	AL	Help for Yak	9	F	10
1	AL	Helping Mr. Ross	9	F	10
1	AL	Trees Can't Run	10	F	10
1	AL	Home Run	10	F	10
1	AL	Under the Warm Sea	12	G	12
1	AL	The Three Wishes	12	G	12
1	AL	A Frog's Life	12	G	12
1	AL	Scarlet's Muffins	12	G	12
1	AL	Joseph Bruchac	14	H	14
1	AL	A New Friend	14	H	14

Grade	Level: Below–, On–, Advanced, ELL	Title	Reading Recovery®	Guided Reading	DRA
1	AL	Congo the Painter	14	H	14
1	AL	Boat Surprise	14	H	14
1	AL	Bobcat Tells a Tale	16	I	16
1	AL	In the Tropics	16	I	16
1	AL	The Missing Bird	16	I	16
1	AL	The Flower Hunt	16	I	16
1	AL	On a Hot Day	18	J	18
1	AL	The Light on the Water	18	J	18
1	AL	How Animals Survive	18	J	18
1	AL	Going Places with Rosy Rabbit	20	J	18
1	AL	Tess Finds at Seabird	20	K	20
1	AL	Billy's Birthday Card	20	K	20
1	AL	The Flying Fish	20	K	20
1	AL	Raccoon and Otter Make Muffins	20	K	20
2	AL	Wendy's Great Catch	20	L	24–28
2	AL	The Surprise by the Stream	20	L	24–28
2	AL	A Pet That Fits	20	L	24–28
2	AL	Hamsters	20	L	24–28
2	AL	Book Week News	20	L	24–28
2	AL	Pelé – Soccer Legend	20	L	24–28
2	AL	A Present for Charlie	20	L	24–28
2	AL	Peacock and Crane	20	L	24–28
2	AL	Rooster's Sore Throat	20	M	24–28
2	AL	Rescue Helicopter	20	M	24–28

Grade	Level: Below–, On–, Advanced, ELL	Title	Reading Recovery®	Guided Reading	DRA
2	AL	On Stage!	20	M	24–28
2	AL	Board Riding: Long Ago and Today	20	M	24–28
2	AL	The Dinosaur Drawing Delivery	20	M	24–28
2	AL	Prairie Babies	20	M	24–28
2	AL	Clues for Grandma	20	M	24–28
2	AL	First Prize	20	N	30
2	AL	Hunter's Secret	20	N	30
2	AL	Music for Everyone	20	N	30
2	AL	Cyrus McCormick: Friend to Farmers	20	N	30
2	AL	What's My Hobby?	20	N	30
2	AL	Happy Again	20	N	30
2	AL	Puppy Tricks	20	N	30
2	AL	The Prairie Dog	22	O	34–38
2	AL	Watching Arctic Wolves	22	O	34–38
2	AL	At the Museum	22	O	34–38
2	AL	Have You Seen Grandma's Panpipe?	22	O	34–38
2	AL	An Artist Named Tomie	22	O	34–38
2	AL	Let's Look for Fossils	22	O	34–38
2	AL	Why Tree Frog Sings at Night	22	O	34–38
2	AL	What a Trip!	22	O	34–38
3	AL	I Am Paige Bridges	22	O	34–38
3	AL	Jana's Eyes	22	O	34–38
3	AL	Guide Dog School	22	O	34–38

Grade	Level: Below–, On–, Advanced, ELL	Title	Reading Recovery®	Guided Reading	DRA
3	AL	Clara Barton: The Angel of the Battlefield	22	P	34–38
3	AL	Science Fair Live!	22	P	34–38
3	AL	Talking Pictures	22	P	34–38
3	AL	Amazing Animal Tales!	22	P	34–38
3	AL	Code Talkers	22	P	34–38
3	AL	The Stonecutter	22	P	34–38
3	AL	The Mother Goose Detective Agency	22	P	34–38
3	AL	Choosing Sides	24	Q	40
3	AL	Trading Places	24	Q	40
3	AL	The Power of Corn	24	Q	40
3	AL	Livingston Hill	24	Q	40
3	AL	Sport Kid Answers Back!	24	Q	40
3	AL	A Tiger at the Door	24	Q	40
3	AL	How Stories Came to Earth: An Ashanti Tale	24	Q	40
3	AL	Mr. Finnigan and Me	24	Q	40
3	AL	Groundhog's New Home	24	Q	40
3	AL	At the Restaurant	24	Q	40
3	AL	The Life of a Pond	24	Q	40
3	AL	Falcons in the Sky	24	R	40
3	AL	Saving Castle Clover	24	R	40
3	AL	Jackson's Book Report	24	R	40
3	AL	The Anywhere Anytime Travel Agency	24	R	40
3	AL	When Pigs Fly	24	R	40
3	AL	Birds and their Nests	24	R	40

Grade	Level: Below–, On–, Advanced, ELL	Title	Reading Recovery®	Guided Reading	DRA
3	AL	Walter and the Food Fair	24	R	40
3	AL	The Sun and the Stars	24	R	40
3	AL	Busy Bees and the *Buzz 12*	24	R	40
K	ELL	How Do You Feel?	1	A	1
K	ELL	My Body	1	A	1
K	ELL	I Like Clothes!	1	A	1
K	ELL	A Family	1	A	1
K	ELL	A Home	2	B	2
K	ELL	What Do Families Do?	1	A	1
K	ELL	Colors at School	1	A	1
K	ELL	Shapes	2	B	2
K	ELL	Numbers	1	A	1
K	ELL	Farm Animals	1	A	1
K	ELL	Food from a Farm	1	A	1
K	ELL	Tools to Grow Things	2	B	2
K	ELL	The Weather	2	B	2
K	ELL	Dress for the Weather	2	B	2
K	ELL	The Seasons	2	B	2
K	ELL	At the Playground	2	B	2
K	ELL	Toys	1	A	1
K	ELL	Let's Play	1	A	1
K	ELL	At the Market	1	A	1
K	ELL	A Neighborhood	2	B	2
K	ELL	At the Park	2	B	2
K	ELL	People Have Jobs	2	B	2
K	ELL	School Workers	2	B	2
K	ELL	Jobs at Home	1	A	1

© Harcourt

Grade	Level: Below–, On–, Advanced, ELL	Title	Reading Recovery®	Guided Reading	DRA
K	ELL	Zoo Animals	1	A	1
K	ELL	Insects	1	A	1
K	ELL	At the Pond	1	A	1
K	ELL	Let's Go!	1	A	1
K	ELL	Places to Go	2	B	2
K	ELL	Be Safe	2	B	2
1	ELL	We Can Help	3	B	2
1	ELL	Lots of Vans	4	B	3
1	ELL	Dad Drives	5	D	4
1	ELL	Jack's Day	6	E	6
1	ELL	My Garden	6	E	6
1	ELL	Up the Hill	7	E	8
1	ELL	Let's Eat!	6	E	6
1	ELL	I Help Clean	7	E	8
1	ELL	Animals Eat Plants	9	F	10
1	ELL	What Game Is It?	10	F	11
1	ELL	A Cold Land	10	F	11
1	ELL	Gold	11	G	12
1	ELL	A Child Grows	11	G	12
1	ELL	The Play	12	G	13
1	ELL	Grandparents	10	F	11
1	ELL	The Big Picture	10	F	11
1	ELL	What Is This Animal?	9	F	10
1	ELL	Snow Play	8	F	10
1	ELL	The Weather	11	G	12
1	ELL	In Joan's City	12	G	13
1	ELL	Our Pet Hamster	12	G	13

Grade	Level: Below-, On-, Advanced, ELL	Title	Reading Recovery®	Guided Reading	DRA
1	ELL	Inside Outside	10	F	11
1	ELL	A Weekend of Fun	11	G	12
1	ELL	Where Is Albert?	12	G	13
1	ELL	Special Animals	12	G	13
1	ELL	Out in Space	13	H	14
1	ELL	At the Beach	11	G	12
1	ELL	At the Car Factory	13	H	14
1	ELL	The Town Garden	13	H	14
1	ELL	Going Shopping	13	H	14
2	ELL	Signs All Around Us	13	H	14
2	ELL	The Fall	13	H	14
2	ELL	Lots of Dogs	13	H	14
2	ELL	Puppy School	13	H	14
2	ELL	I Read the TV News	13	H	14
2	ELL	Let's Play Sports	13	H	14
2	ELL	All About Bikes	15	I	16
2	ELL	Many Kinds of Birds	15	I	16
2	ELL	Down on the Farm	15	I	16
2	ELL	The Firefighter	15	I	16
2	ELL	Art in the Subway	15	I	16
2	ELL	Toys: Long Ago and Today	15	I	16
2	ELL	Just Like Olivia	15	I	16
2	ELL	Rain Forest Homes	15	I	16
2	ELL	A Birthday Surprise	15	I	16
2	ELL	Katie's Book	18	J	18–20
2	ELL	Guitar Lessons	18	J	18–20

© Harcourt

Grade	Level: Below–, On–, Advanced, ELL	Title	Reading Recovery®	Guided Reading	DRA
2	ELL	It's Fun to Dance	20	L	24–28
2	ELL	Peanuts	20	L	24–28
2	ELL	The Art of Sculpture	20	K	24–28
2	ELL	In Our Neighborhood	20	K	24–28
2	ELL	Farmer Bert	20	K	24–28
2	ELL	Insects	20	L	24–28
2	ELL	A Wild Animal Tour	20	L	24–28
2	ELL	My Community	20	M	24–28
2	ELL	Food Around the World	20	M	24–28
2	ELL	I Love to Write	20	M	24–28
2	ELL	Collecting Seashells	20	M	24–28
2	ELL	Reptiles	20	M	24–28
2	ELL	My Travel Journal	20	M	24–28
3	ELL	Friends	20	L	24–28
3	ELL	Nathan and His Favorite Author	20	L	24–28
3	ELL	A New School for Chris	20	L	24–28
3	ELL	Astronauts	20	M	24–28
3	ELL	Today's News	20	M	24–28
3	ELL	Let's Play	20	M	24–28
3	ELL	Helping Out	20	N	30
3	ELL	Animals All Around Us	20	N	30
3	ELL	Alex Bakes a Cake	20	N	30
3	ELL	The Most Important Meal of the Day	20	N	30
3	ELL	Baby Brother	20	N	30
3	ELL	The Country of Chile	20	N	30
3	ELL	Our Backyard	20	N	30

© Harcourt

Grade	Level: Below–, On–, Advanced, ELL	Title	Reading Recovery®	Guided Reading	DRA
3	ELL	The Parts of a Tree	20	N	30
3	ELL	Answer This!	20	N	30
3	ELL	The Three Little Pigs	20	N	30
3	ELL	Bears Everywhere	20	N	30
3	ELL	Mark's Memories	20	N	30
3	ELL	The Deer and the Quail	22	O	34–38
3	ELL	Let's Put on a Play	22	O	34–38
3	ELL	Water, Ice, and Snow	22	O	34–38
3	ELL	Animals at Night	22	O	34–38
3	ELL	How a City Works	22	O	34–38
3	ELL	School Rules!	22	O	34–38
3	ELL	Rory the Robot	22	O	34–38
3	ELL	Pigs in Our World	22	O	34–38
3	ELL	Patterns in Our World	22	O	34–38
3	ELL	How Scientists Work	22	O	34–38
3	ELL	Our Planet Earth	22	P	34–38
3	ELL	Star Light, Star Bright	22	P	34–38

© Harcourt

Individual Reading Inventories

Introduction

An Individual Reading Inventory (IRI) is an assessment tool to help a teacher track a child's strengths and weaknesses and to help plan instruction accordingly. An IRI has two primary parts: a reading passage and comprehension questions.

Administering the Individual Reading Inventory

1. Before reading, explain the task. Tell the child that he or she will read a passage aloud and then answer five questions.

2. During reading, record oral miscues—both meaning-based and graphic/sound-based—on the Individual Reading Inventory Form. Use the Marking Oral Reading Miscues chart on page 34 as a guide to identify and record errors.

3. After reading, ask the child the questions at the end of the Individual Reading Inventory Form. Mark correct (+) and incorrect (–) responses.

Assessing Performance

In some cases, it will be necessary to decide whether to count a mispronunciation or another minor miscue as an error. For example, most teachers do not hold children responsible for mispronouncing unfamiliar proper names. Likewise, miscues that do not affect the meaning may be considered unimportant (for example, when a child reads *bike* for *bicycle*).

Miscues

Total the number of miscues and compute the Error Rate. Then follow the steps on the Individual Reading Inventory Summary Form on page 44. Look for an Error Rate of 10% or less to confirm instructional reading level; 5% or less for independent reading level.

© Harcourt

Error Rate

1. Total the number of miscues.

2. Divide this number by the word count of the passage.

Comprehension

Total the number of correct responses to the questions. Look for a score of 80% or higher to confirm instructional reading level. To help evaluate comprehension errors, questions 1–3 require literal thinking; questions 4–5 require inferential thinking.

CONVERSION TABLE*

Percent Accuracy	Reading Level
95–100	Independent
90–94	Instructional
50–89	Frustration

* All percentages are approximate and should be combined with teacher judgment.

Oral Reading Fluency Assessment

What Is Oral Reading Fluency?

Research recognizes fluency as a strong indicator of efficient and proficient reading. A fluent reader reads orally with accuracy and expression, at a speech-like pace. Oral reading fluency is an assessment of accuracy and rate. It is expressed as the number of words read correctly per minute (WCPM).

Reading researchers have demonstrated the importance of "automaticity," or reading automatically. If a reader devotes most of his or her attention to pronouncing words, comprehension and meaning will suffer. On the other hand, children who read fluently can devote more attention to meaning and thus increase their comprehension. This is why oral reading fluency is an important goal of reading instruction, especially in the elementary grades.

Assessing oral reading fluency helps a teacher determine how well a child can apply decoding skills and recognize high-frequency words. It also helps a teacher plan instruction in word analysis and evaluate the effects of special instruction designed to improve decoding skills.

Choosing a Passage

To test a child's oral reading fluency, select part of a reading passage from a Leveled Reader. You have two options—

- Choose a passage from this book, a passage which the child has not yet read.

- Choose a passage from another Leveled Reader.

In either case, count the words in the passage to determine that they meet the minimum requirements for a child at that grade and time of year. See the chart on page 33 as a guide. The passage should be long enough to allow the child to score in the 90th percentile. For example, a child in the second grade in mid-year (winter) should read a passage that contains a minimum of 125 words in a minute.

Administering Oral Reading Fluency Assessment

Use a stopwatch or the second hand of a watch or clock to time readers for one minute. While the child is reading, make a check mark above a word whenever you hear a reading error. Reading errors include omissions, mispronunciations, and substitutions. (Do not count repetitions or self-corrections as errors.) When you reach the one minute mark, place a slash mark after the last word the child has read. This will give you the child's total words read in a minute. Count the number of errors and subtract this amount from the total number of words read in a minute. This will give you a final score—the number of words correct per minute (WCPM).

Hasbrouck & Tindal
Oral Reading Fluency Data

Grade	Percentile	Fall WCPM*	Winter WCPM*	Spring WCPM*	Avg. Weekly Improvement**
1	90		81	111	1.9
	75		47	82	2.2
	50		23	53	1.9
	25		12	28	1.0
	10		6	15	0.6
2	90	106	125	142	1.1
	75	79	100	117	1.2
	50	51	72	89	1.2
	25	25	42	61	1.1
	10	11	18	31	0.6
3	90	128	146	162	1.1
	75	99	120	137	1.2
	50	71	92	107	1.1
	25	44	62	78	1.1
	10	21	36	48	0.8

* WCPM: Words Correct Per Minute
** Average words per week growth

© Harcourt

Marking Oral Reading Miscues

READING MISCUE	MARKING
1. omission (error)	Circle the word that the child omits or the teacher supplies. I will let you (go) in.
2. insertion (error)	Insert a caret (^), and write in the inserted word. We bought a ^big parrot.
3. substitution (error)	Write the word the child substitutes over the word in the text. If there are multiple attempts to read a word, only one error should be counted. Dad fixed ~~my~~ the bike.
4. mispronunciation (error)	Write the phonetic mispronunciation over the word. Have you ~~fed~~ feed the dog?
5. self-correction (not an error)	Write the letters SC next to the miscue that is self-corrected and is no longer an error. We took our ~~spote~~ space. SC
6. repetition (not an error)	Draw a line under any part of the text that is repeated. It is your garden now.
7. punctuation (not an error)	Circle punctuation missed. Write in any punctuation inserted. "Are you home(.)" said Frank. ?
8. hesitation (not an error)	Place vertical lines at places where the child hesitates excessively. Pretend|this is mine.

© Harcourt

Scoring Rubric for Retelling Fiction

Score of 4	The child: • names and describes the main and supporting characters and tells how they change or learn • tells about the setting • describes the problems and resolutions in the story • uses vocabulary, sentence structure, or literary devices from the story • accurately describes the theme or meaning of the story • provides extensions of the story such as making connections to other texts, relating relevant experiences, and/or making generalizations • requires little or no prompting
Score of 3	The child: • names and describes the main characters • tells about the setting • describes some of the problems and resolutions in the story • uses some vocabulary or literary devices from the story • relates some aspects of the theme or meaning of the story • provides some extensions of the story such as making connections to other texts or relating relevant experiences • may require some prompting
Score of 2	The child: • tells some details about the story elements, including characters, setting, and plot, with some omissions or errors • uses little language and vocabulary from story • shows minimal understanding of the theme or meaning • provides minimal extensions of the story • requires some prompting to retell the story
Score of 1	The child: • tells few if any details about the story elements, possibly with errors • has little or no awareness of the theme of the story • provides no extensions of the story • is unable to retell the story without prompting

© Harcourt

Scoring Rubric for Retelling Nonfiction

Score of 4	The child: • relates the main idea and important supporting details • stays on topic • understands text features such as cause and effect, chronological order, classifying, grouping, or compare and contrast • discriminates between fact and fiction • uses vocabulary or sentence structure from the text • clearly tells the conclusion or point of the text with detail • identifies the author's purpose • makes connections to relevant texts, experiences, and/or generalizations • requires little or no prompting
Score of 3	The child: • relates the main idea and relevant details • mostly stays on topic • mostly understands text features such as cause and effect, chronological order, classifying, grouping, or comparing • discriminates between fact and fiction • uses some vocabulary from the text • tells the conclusion or point of the text • identifies the author's purpose • makes connections to other texts or relates relevant experiences • may require some prompting
Score of 2	The child: • shows minimal understanding of main idea and omits important details • might stray from topic • understands few, if any, text features • uses little or no vocabulary from the text • does not fully understand conclusion or point of the text • shows some awareness of author's purpose • provides few, if any, extensions of the text • requires some prompting to retell the story
Score of 1	The child: • shows no understanding of main idea and omits important details • does not understand or recognize text features • does not understand conclusion of the text • provides no extensions of the text • is unable to retell the story without prompting

© Harcourt

Observational Checklist, Kindergarten
Reading Behaviors

Child's Name: _____

Administer the Observational Checklist three times during the school year—beginning, middle, and end—to monitor a child's developing familiarity with books and written language. Each time you assess the child, fill in the date and the proficiency level demonstrated—either 1, 2, or 3—as described by the scale below.

Rating Scale:
1 = Shows no evidence of this behavior
2 = Shows some evidence of this behavior
3 = Shows substantial evidence of this behavior

Performance Level:
Entry-level
Emerging
Proficient

Behavior	Child's Rating		
	Date	Date	Date
Recognizes types of everyday print (signs, books, labels, poems, lists)			
Recognizes own name in print			
Enjoys listening to stories, books, poems read aloud			
Participates in shared reading activities			
Voluntarily looks at books			
Handles a book correctly (holds right side up, turns pages, etc.)			
Recalls details from familiar stories (characters, setting, important events)			
Retells familiar stories in a logical order			
Responds to stories through discussions and interpretive activities (art, drama, etc.)			
Connects characters, events, and information in books read aloud to life experiences			
Distinguishes fantasy from realistic stories			
Retells own stories			
Recognizes that print contains meaning			
Recognizes that sentences in print are made up of separate words			
Tracks print—from left-to-right and top-to-bottom			
Matches all consonants and short-vowel sounds to appropriate letters			
Understands that as letters of words change, so do the sounds (alphabetic principle)			
Reads simple one-syllable words and high-frequency words			
Identifies and sorts words (e.g., colors, shapes, foods)			
Reads simple sentences			

Comments _____
_____
_____

© Harcourt

Observational Checklist, Grade 1
Reading Behaviors

Child's Name: _____

Administer the Observational Checklist three times during the school year—beginning, middle, and end—to monitor a child's developing familiarity with books and written language. Each time you assess the child, fill in the date and the proficiency level demonstrated—either 1, 2, or 3—as described by the scale below.

Rating Scale:
1 = Shows no evidence of this behavior
2 = Shows some evidence of this behavior
3 = Shows substantial evidence of this behavior

Performance Level:
Entry-level
Emerging
Proficient

Behavior	Child's Rating		
	Date	Date	Date
Applies basic letter-sound correspondences to decode regularly spelled words			
Learns and applies structural cues to decode and recognize words: compounds, base words, inflections, contractions			
Uses letter-sound correspondences and spelling patterns to recognize or sound out unknown words			
Uses letter-sound knowledge, word order, language structure, and context to recognize words			
Recognizes high-frequency words in and out of context			
Develops and expands vocabulary through listening			
Sorts, classifies, and identifies related words			
Identifies synonyms, antonyms, and multiple-meaning words			
Uses title and illustrations to make predictions; reads to confirm			
Retells and sequences story events			
Identifies and recalls details, events, and ideas of familiar stories			
Analyzes characters' traits, feelings, and relationships			
Produces artwork and writing to reflect understanding of text			
Relates reading to personal experiences and knowledge			
Uses end punctuation and quotation marks as clues to meaning			
Summarizes the main idea			
Notices when reading fails to make sense and begins to self-correct			
Draws visual images based on text content			
Determines purpose for reading; discusses purpose of text			
Connects, compares, and contrasts characters and topics across texts			
Distinguishes reality from fantasy			
Completes story maps and graphic organizers			
Reads aloud with accuracy and comprehension			
Self-selects books and reads independently on a regular basis			
Draws and explains inferences, important ideas, causes-effects, predictions, and conclusions			

Comments _____

_____

_____

© Harcourt

Observational Checklist, Grade 2
Reading Behaviors

Child's Name: _____

Administer the Observational Checklist three times during the school year—beginning, middle, and end—to monitor a child's developing familiarity with books and written language. Each time you assess the child, fill in the date and the proficiency level demonstrated—either 1, 2, or 3—as described by the scale below.

Rating Scale:
1 = Shows no evidence of this behavior
2 = Shows some evidence of this behavior
3 = Shows substantial evidence of this behavior

Performance Level:
Entry-level
Emerging
Proficient

Behavior	Child's Rating		
	Date	Date	Date
Applies basic and complex letter-sound correspondences to decode words			
Learns and applies structural cues to decode and recognize compound words, base words, inflections, contractions, prefixes, and suffixes			
Decodes multisyllable words using letter-sound correspondences and spelling patterns			
Uses word order, language structure, and context to support word identification or to confirm meaning			
Recognizes high-frequency words in and out of context			
Expands vocabulary through listening and reading			
Sorts, classifies, and identifies related words			
Recognizes word relationships, synonyms, antonyms, multiple-meaning words, homophones, and homographs			
Consults dictionary and reference sources to build meaning			
Uses title and illustrations to make predictions; reads to confirm			
Retells and sequences story events; produces summary of text selections			
Identifies and recalls main idea, characters, events, setting, problem, and solution from text			
Analyzes characters' traits, feelings, and relationships			
Produces artwork and writing to reflect understanding of text			
Relates reading to own experiences and knowledge before and during after reading			
Uses punctuation as clues to meaning			
Produces summaries of text selections			
Monitors own reading and self-corrects using strategies: rereading, searching for clues, asking for help, and self-questioning			
Draws visual images based on text content			
Determines purpose for reading; identifies purpose of text			
Connects, compares, and contrasts characters and topics across texts			
Distinguishes reality from fantasy and fiction from nonfiction and fact			
Represents text in a variety of ways			
Reads aloud with accuracy and comprehension			
Self-selects reading materials based on interests, knowledge of authors, illustrators, and difficulty			
Draws and explains inferences, important ideas, causes-effects, predictions, and conclusions			

Comments _____
_____
_____

© Harcourt

Observational Checklist, Grade 3
Reading Behaviors

Student's Name: _____

Administer the Observational Checklist three times during the school year—beginning, middle, and end—to monitor a student's developing familiarity with books and written language. Each time you assess the student, fill in the date and the proficiency level demonstrated—either 1, 2, or 3—as described by the scale below.

Rating Scale:
1 = Shows no evidence of this behavior
2 = Shows some evidence of this behavior
3 = Shows substantial evidence of this behavior

Performance Level:
Entry-level
Emerging
Proficient

Behavior	Student's Rating		
	Date	Date	Date
Applies basic and complex letter-sound correspondences to decode words			
Applies structural cues to decode and recognize compound words, base words, inflections, contractions, prefixes, suffixes, and letter, spelling, and syllable patterns			
Decodes multisyllable words using letter-sound correspondences and spelling and syllable patterns			
Uses word order, language structure, and context to support word identification or to confirm meaning			
Recognizes high-frequency words in and out of context			
Expands vocabulary through listening, reading, and writing			
Sorts, classifies, and identifies related words			
Recognizes word relationships: synonyms, antonyms, multiple-meaning words, homophones, and homographs			
Consults dictionary and reference sources to build meaning			
Uses title, illustrations, and prior knowledge to hypothesize and predict content; reads to confirm			
Identifies and recalls main idea, characters, events, setting, problem, solution, and sequence of events from text			
Analyzes characters' traits, feeling, and relationships			
Produces artwork and writing to reflect understanding of text and to extend meaning			
Uses prior knowledge to anticipate, construct, and confirm meaning			
Uses punctuation as clues to meaning			
Produces summaries of text selections			
Monitors own reading and self-corrects using strategies: rereading, searching for clues, asking for help, self-questioning, reading aloud, and using references/resources			
Draws visual images based on text content			
Establishes and adjusts purpose for reading; identifies purpose of text			
Connects, compares, and contrasts characters, topics, and themes across texts			
Distinguishes between reality-fantasy, fact-opinion, and fiction-nonfiction			
Represents text in a variety of ways			
Reads aloud with accuracy and comprehension			
Self-selects reading materials based on interests, knowledge of authors, illustrators, and difficulty			
Draws and explains inferences, important ideas, causes-effects, predictions, and conclusions			
Recognizes point of view			
Recognizes use of literary devices			

Comments _____

_____

Concepts About Print Inventory

Child's Name: _____

The Concepts About Print Inventory is designed for children who have not yet learned to read independently. It is a less formal method of assessment that will give a teacher insight into a child's literacy experiences. It will help you determine whether the child is aware of the functions of reading and writing and whether the child has been read to very much. It will also help you see how familiar the child is with books, written language, and the conventions of print.

The Concepts About Print Inventory may be administered three times during the school year—beginning, middle, and end—to monitor a child's developing familiarity with books and written language. Each time you assess the child, fill in the date and the proficiency level demonstrated—either 1, 2, or 3—as described by the scale below.

Rating Scale:
1 = Shows no evidence of this behavior
2 = Shows some evidence of this behavior
3 = Shows substantial evidence of this behavior

Performance Level:
Entry-level
Emerging
Proficient

Behavior Assessed	Date	Date	Date
1. Parts of book: Can the child identify the front of a book, the back of a book, and the title page?			
2. Title, author, and illustrator: Can the child identify the title of a book? Does the child know what an author is? Does the child know what an illustrator does?			
3. Purpose of print: Does the child know that print represents language? Does the child know that one reads print?			
4. Left-to-right direction: Does the child understand that one reads left to right?			
5. Return sweep: Does the child understand what a reader should do when he or she reaches the end of a line of print?			
6. Letter: Can the child identify a letter? Can the child recognize an uppercase letter and a lowercase letter?			
7. Word: Can the child identify a word?			
8. Punctuation (period): Does the child understand the purpose of a period?			
9. Punctuation (question mark): Does the child understand the purpose of a question mark?			

Comments _____

_____

Phonemic Awareness Inventory

Child's Name: _____

The Phonemic Awareness Inventory may be administered three times during the school year—beginning, middle, and end—to monitor a child's developing familiarity with language. Each time you assess the child, fill in the date and the proficiency level demonstrated—either 1, 2, or 3—as described by the scale below

Rating Scale:

1 = Shows no knowledge of this concept

2 = Shows some knowledge of this concept

3 = Shows substantial knowledge of this concept

Performance Level:

Entry-level

Emerging

Proficient

Behavior Assessed	Date	Date	Date
1. Produces rhyming sounds			
2. Matches beginning sounds			
3. Isolates beginning sounds			
4. Blends syllables			
5. Blends onset-rimes and phonemes			
6. Segments words in a sentence and segments syllables in a word			
7. Segments phonemes in a word			
8. Avoids deleting words and syllables			
9. Avoids deleting phonemes			
10. Avoids substituting initial and final sounds			

Comments _____

_____

_____

Phonics Inventory

Child's Name: _____

The Phonics Inventory may be administered three times during the school year—beginning, middle, and end—to monitor a child's developing familiarity with language. Each time you assess the child, fill in the date and the proficiency level demonstrated—either 1, 2, or 3—as described by the scale below.

Rating Scale:
1 = Shows no knowledge of this concept
2 = Shows some knowledge of this concept
3 = Shows substantial knowledge of this concept

Performance Level:
Entry-level
Emerging
Proficient

Behavior Assessed	Date	Date	Date
CVC Words—Identifies: • initial consonants and single consonants • short medial vowels • final single consonants and consonant blends			
Consonant Blends—Identifies: • initial consonants and consonant blends • short medial vowels • final single consonants and consonant blends			
Consonant Digraphs—Identifies: • initial consonant digraph • final consonant digraphs • short medial vowels			
CVCe Words—Identifies: • long vowels in the CVCe pattern • initial single consonants • final single consonants			
Vowels—Identifies: • vowel digraphs • vowel dipthongs • r-controlled vowels			
Multisyllabic Words—Identifies: • short vowels in closed syllables (e.g., "dab") • long vowels in open syllables (e.g., "ta") • inflections, prefixes, and suffixes			

Comments _____

_____

_____

Individual Reading Inventory Summary Form

Child: _____ Date: _____

Passage: _____ Word Count: _____

Calculate the Error Rate:

Miscues

Meaning-based miscues: _____

Graphic/sound-based miscues: _____

Total number of miscues: _____

Divide the total number of miscues by the word count of the passage.

_____ ÷ _____ = _____

   miscues   word count   error rate

Calculate the Comprehension Score

_____ × 20 = _____%

  total correct answers   comprehension score

Comments _____

_____

_____

Calculate the Fluency Rate:

_____ ÷ _____ = _____

   WCPM   word count   fluency rate

(number of correct
words read per minute)

Grade __K__ **Level** __OL__

Reader's Name: _____ **Date:** _____

Title and Author: _*Come In the Barn* by Michele Perreault_

Word Count: ____24____

Number of Errors: Word Recognition _____ Comprehension _____

Meets Benchmark: Yes _____ No _____

Before Reading

Introduce the book:
In this story, Tim and Sis lead animals into a barn. Read to find out which animals go inside. Then I will ask you some questions.

After Reading

Ask the following comprehension questions:

(+ or –)

☐	1.	**Which animal goes into the barn first?** (pig)
☐	2.	**Which animal goes into the barn last?** (cat)
☐	3.	**Who calls the animals into the barn?** (Tim and Sis)

Individual Reading Inventory

Come in, pig.	3
Come in, horse.	6
Come in, cow.	9
Come in, hen.	12
Come in, dog.	15
Come in, cat.	18
Come in, Tim.	21
Come in, Sis.	24

Comments _____

_____

_____

_____

Grade K **Level** AL

Reader's Name: _____ **Date:** _____

Title and Author: _*I Like What I See* by Morgan Pierce_

Word Count: ___43___

Number of Errors: Word Recognition _____ Comprehension _____

Meets Benchmark: Yes _____ No _____

Before Reading

Introduce the book:
In this story, children are visiting a farm. A farmer shows them around. Read to find out what they see on the farm. Then I will ask you some questions.

After Reading

Ask the following comprehension questions:

(+ or −)

☐ 1. **What is the cat doing in the story?** (taking a nap)

☐ 2. **Which animal sips in the story?** (cow)

☐ 3. **Where does the story take place?** (on a farm)

Individual Reading Inventory

Come here.	2
You will like what you see.	8
Come see a cat nap.	13
Come see a pig dig.	18
Come see a cow sip.	23
Come see a dog kiss.	28
Do you like what you see?	34
We do like it.	38
We like what we see.	43

Comments _____

_____

_____

_____

Grade ___K___ **Level** ___OL___

Reader's Name: _____ Date: _____

Title and Author: _____*We Want a Pet* by Winston White_____

Word Count: ___48___

Number of Errors: Word Recognition _____ Comprehension _____

Meets Benchmark: Yes _____ No _____

Before Reading

Introduce the book:
In this story, a child and his dad are choosing a pet at the pet store. Read to find out which pet they choose. Then I will ask you some questions.

After Reading

Ask the following comprehension questions:

(+ or −)

☐ 1. **Which kind of pet can hop?** (a rabbit)

☐ 2. **Which kind of pet has a bell?** (a cat)

☐ 3. **Which pet does the child choose? Why?** (a dog; because it is friendly and wags its tails)

Individual Reading Inventory

We want to get a pet.	6
Look at this pet.	10
This pet can get wet.	15
Look at this pet.	19
This pet can hop.	23
Look at this pet.	27
It is not big.	31
Look at this pet.	35
This pet has a bell.	40
We want this pet.	44
This pet can wag!	48

Comments _____

_____

_____

_____

Grade ___K___ Level ___AL___

Reader's Name: _____ Date: _____

Title and Author: _*The Pet for Us* by Casey McLaughlin_

Word Count: ___61___

Number of Errors: Word Recognition _____ Comprehension _____

Meets Benchmark: Yes _____ No _____

Before Reading

Introduce the book:
In this story, two children visit a pet store. Read to find out which kind of pet the children choose. Then I will ask you some questions. (Have the child read pages 5 through 8.)

After Reading

Ask the following comprehension questions:

(+ or –)

☐	1. **Why don't the children like the mouse?** (It is little.)
☐	2. **Why don't the children like the dog?** (It is big.)
☐	3. **Which pet do the children choose?** (a cat)

Individual Reading Inventory

We do not want a mouse.	6
It is not a good pet for us.	14
It is little.	17
Do you like this dog?	22
Is this a good pet for you?	29
A dog is not the pet we want.	37
We do not want a dog.	43
It is big.	46
We like this cat.	50
We want to get it.	55
This is the pet for us!	61

Comments _____

_____

_____

_____

Grade __K__ **Level** __BL__

Reader's Name: _____ Date: _____

Title and Author: _*Letters and Sounds, Review 2* by Kyle Stillwell_

Word Count: __31__

Number of Errors: Word Recognition _____ Comprehension _____

Meets Benchmark: Yes _____ No _____

Before Reading

Introduce the book:
In this story, a moving van takes things from one house to another house. Read to find out what goes inside the van. Then I will ask you some questions.

After Reading

Ask the following comprehension questions:

(+ or −)

☐ 1. **Who is Ken?** (the family dog)

☐ 2. **What things are put in the van?** (bed, box, rug, pot, Ken)

☐ 3. **Why are things put in the van?** (The family is moving.)

Individual Reading Inventory

The big van is here.	5
Will the bed fit?	9
Will the box fit?	13
Will the rug fit?	17
Will the pot fit?	21
Ken will go in the van.	27
The van is here.	31

Comments _____

_____

_____

Grade ___K___ Level ___OL___

Reader's Name: _____ Date: _____

Title and Author: ___*Pam and Hal* by Cadie Higgins___

Word Count: ___60___

Number of Errors: Word Recognition _____ Comprehension _____

Meets Benchmark: Yes _____ No _____

Before Reading

Introduce the book:

In this story, Hal and Pam are climbing a big hill. Read to find out if they make it to the top. Then I will ask you some questions. (Have the child begin on page 3 with "Hal will huff" and read to page 7, stopping after "a lot to look at.")

After Reading

Ask the following comprehension questions:

(+ or −)

☐ 1. **Do Hal and Pam get to the top?** (yes)

☐ 2. **What do Hal and Pam do when they get to the top?** (They sit and look down.)

☐ 3. **How do Hal and Pam get to the top?** (They don't quit.)

© Harcourt

Individual Reading Inventory

Hal will huff and puff.	5
Pam will huff and puff.	10
Will they get to the top?	16
Will they quit?	19
Hal will not quit.	23
Pam will not quit.	27
They want to get to the top.	34
Hal and Pam get to the top.	41
They will sit and look down.	47
Look at what they can see.	53
They have a lot to look at.	60

Comments _____

_____

_____

Grade __K__ Level __AL__

Reader's Name: _____ **Date:** _____

Title and Author: _____ *Ben Has to Go!* by Samantha Montgomery _____

Word Count: ____67____

Number of Errors: Word Recognition _____ Comprehension _____

Meets Benchmark: Yes _____ No _____

Before Reading

Introduce the book:
In this story, Ben has to get to a show. Read to find out how he and his friend Sid get there. Then I will ask you some questions. (Have the child begin at the bottom of page 4 at "A cab will not come" and read to the end of page 7.)

After Reading

Ask the following comprehension questions:

(+ or −)

☐ 1. **Who is going to the show?** (Ben and Sid)

☐ 2. **What do Ben and Sid take to the show?** (a bus)

☐ 3. **Why don't Ben and Sid ride in a cab?** (because a cab will not come)

Individual Reading Inventory

A cab will not come.	5
What can Ben and Sid do?	11
Ben can see a bus.	16
"The bus will get us there," said Ben.	24
"Hop in!" said the man in the bus.	32
"We are Ben and Sid," said Ben.	39
"Ben has to play in a show," said Sid.	48
"Can you get us there?" said Ben.	55
"Yes, I can," said the man.	61
"This bus will get you there."	67

Comments _____

_____

_____

_____

Grade __1__ Level __BL__

© Harcourt

Reader's Name: _____ Date: _____

Title and Author: _____*Use Your Feet!* by Di Pert_____

Word Count: ____35____

Number of Errors: Word Recognition _____ Comprehension _____

Meets Benchmark: Yes _____ No _____

Before Reading

Introduce the book:
In this story, Grant plays games and runs. Read to find out what he can do. Then I will ask you some questions.

After Reading

Ask the following comprehension questions:

(+ or −)

☐ 1. **Who is the story about?** (Grant)

☐ 2. **Which parts of his body does Grant use?** (feet, head, arms)

☐ 3. **How far can Grant run?** (He can run a long way.)

☐ 4. **When does this story happen? How do you know?** (It happens during recess or after school; I know because the bell rings at school.)

☐ 5. **Why does Grant run every day at his school?** (He likes running.)

Individual Reading Inventory

The bell rings at school.	5
Use your arms, Grant!	9
Use your head, Grant!	13
Use your feet, Grant!	17
Grant's feet can go fast.	22
He runs a long way.	27
Now Grant runs at his school every day.	35

Comments _____

_____

_____

© Harcourt

Grade _1_ **Level** _OL_

© Harcourt

Reader's Name: _____ **Date:** _____

Title and Author: _*Cliff's Feet* by Di Pert_____

Word Count: _63_____

Number of Errors: Word Recognition _____ Comprehension _____

Meets Benchmark: Yes _____ No _____

Before Reading

Introduce the book:
In this book, Cliff wants to try something new. Read to find out what he tries. Then I will ask you some questions.

After Reading

Ask the following comprehension questions:

(+ or −)

☐ 1. **What does Cliff do at school?** (He runs fast and jumps a long way.)

☐ 2. **What does Cliff miss every time?** (the ball)

☐ 3. **Who tells Cliff to use his feet to swim?** (Liz)

☐ 4. **Which thing is Cliff good at?** (swimming)

☐ 5. **Why can Cliff swim fast?** (He has long feet.)

Individual Reading Inventory

Cliff has long feet.	4
At school, he runs fast and jumps a long way.	14
Cliff wants to do a new thing.	21
At home, Liz says, "Use your arms to swing."	30
"I can't hit the ball," says Cliff.	37
"Use your head," says Liz.	42
"I miss the ball every time," says Cliff.	50
"Use your feet to swim," says Liz.	57
"I can swim fast!" says Cliff.	63

Comments _____

_____

_____

_____

© Harcourt

Grade 1 **Level** AL

Reader's Name: _____ **Date:** _____

Title and Author: *Home Run* by Di Pert _____

Word Count: _____73_____

Number of Errors: Word Recognition _____ Comprehension _____

Meets Benchmark: Yes _____ No _____

Before Reading

Introduce the book:
In this story, Sam is seeing which sport Ming plays well.
Read to find out what happens. Then I will ask you some
questions. (Have the child read pages 4 through 8.)

After Reading

Ask the following comprehension questions:

(+ or –)

☐ 1. **Where does Ming try to toss the ball?** (in the net)

☐ 2. **What does Ming do with the ball?** (She throws it over the net.)

☐ 3. **How does Ming feel when she misses the net?** (She feels sad.)

☐ 4. **Which game is Ming good at?** (baseball)

☐ 5. **How does Sam know Ming is good at hitting a ball with a bat?** (She hits a home run every time.)

Individual Reading Inventory

"Can you toss the ball in the net?" asked Sam.	10
Ming jumped with the ball.	15
The ball went way up past the net.	23
Ming looked down at her feet.	29
"It's no good," she said.	34
"I can't get the ball in the net."	42
Sam got a bat and a ball.	49
"Use your arms, Ming!" says Sam.	55
Ming swung the bat.	59
"You are good at this," said Sam.	66
"You hit a home run every time!"	73

Comments _____

_____

_____

_____

Grade ___1___ Level ___BL___

Reader's Name: _____ Date: _____

Title and Author: _*In the Desert* by Penny Lee Forest_

Word Count: ___79___

Number of Errors: Word Recognition _____ Comprehension _____

Meets Benchmark: Yes _____ No _____

Before Reading

Introduce the book:
This book is about the desert. Read to find out about the people and animals who live there. Then I will ask you some questions.

After Reading

Ask the following comprehension questions:

(+ or –)

[ ] **1. Who lives in the desert?** (people, animals)

[ ] **2. What do people in the deserts live in?** (houses made of mud, tents)

[ ] **3. What is the weather like in a desert?** (dry, with very little rain; it can be hot or cold)

[ ] **4. Why do you think people in deserts move from place to place?** (to find food and water)

[ ] **5. Why do tents in the desert have holes on top?** (to let in air for people to breathe)

© Harcourt

Individual Reading Inventory

A desert is a dry place. Very little rain falls.	10
A desert can be hot or cold.	17
This desert is hot. People put on things to	26
stay cool.	28
This desert is cold. People put on things to	37
stay warm.	39
Some people live in houses. The four	46
sides are made of mud.	51
Some people live in tents. They move	58
from place to place. The tents have holes in	67
the top to let in air.	73
Animals live in the desert, too.	79

Comments _____

_____

_____

_____

Grade <u>1</u>   **Level** <u>OL</u>

Reader's Name: _____   **Date:** _____

Title and Author: _____*In the Snow* by Penny Lee Forest_____

Word Count: _____86_____

Number of Errors: Word Recognition _____ Comprehension _____

Meets Benchmark: Yes _____ No _____

Before Reading

Introduce the book:
This story is about people who live in a place with a lot of snow. Read to find out more. Then I will ask you some questions. (Have the child begin on page 3 and stop at "still like to fish" on page 7.)

After Reading

Ask the following comprehension questions:

(+ or –)

- [ ] 1. **What did the people use to make houses long ago?** (snow and ice)

- [ ] 2. **How did the people move across the snow?** (in dog sleds)

- [ ] 3. **Why did the people cut holes in the ice?** (to fish)

- [ ] 4. **What changed about how the people live?** (They no longer live in houses made of snow.)

- [ ] 5. **What stayed the same?** (They still like to fish.)

Individual Reading Inventory

A long time ago, some people made their	8
houses out of snow and ice. The ice kept the cool	19
air out. It also kept the warm air in.	28
The people fished. They would cut holes in the	37
ice. Then they would wait for the fish to come.	47
The people used dog sleds like these to	55
move across the snow. This sled has four dogs	64
pulling it.	66
Today people still live in warm houses. The	74
houses are not made of snow.	80
The people still like to fish.	86

Comments _____

_____

_____

_____

Grade _1_ **Level** _AL_

Reader's Name: _____ Date: _____

Title and Author: _*In the Tropics* by Penny Lee Forest_

Word Count: _89_

Number of Errors: Word Recognition _____ Comprehension _____

Meets Benchmark: Yes _____ No _____

Before Reading

Introduce the book:
Read this book to find out how people live in the tropics.
Then I will ask you some questions. (Have the child begin
on page 5 and read through to the end of page 8.)

After Reading

Ask the following comprehension questions:

(+ or –)

☐ 1. **Which kind of forest is in the tropics?** (rain forest)

☐ 2. **Which kinds of houses do people in the tropics live in?** (huts, houses on stilts, tall buildings)

☐ 3. **What are the houses in the tropics made of?** (trees, leaves, sticks and plants)

☐ 4. **What do all people in the tropics need?** (to stay cool and dry)

☐ 5. **How do people in the tropics stay dry?** (Some people live in houses on stilts; they stay under shelter when it rains.)

Individual Reading Inventory

There are many rain forests in the tropics.   8

Some people live in the rain forest. These   16

people live in huts. The huts are made   24

from trees and leaves.   28

    Some people in the tropics live in   35

houses on stilts. These houses are made   42

from sticks and plants. When there is   49

a lot of rain, the houses stay dry.   57

    Some people in the tropics live in tall   65

buildings. In the buildings, the air   71

is cool.   73

    People live in different ways in the tropics.   81

They all need to stay cool and dry.   89

Comments _____

_____

_____

Reader's Name: _____ **Date:** _____

Title and Author: *Hedgehog and Beaver Have a Picnic* by A.M. Jackson

Word Count: ___111___

Number of Errors: Word Recognition _____ Comprehension _____

Meets Benchmark: Yes _____ No _____

Before Reading

Introduce the book:
Read this story to find out how Hedgehog and Beaver pack for a picnic. Then I will ask you some questions. (Have the child begin on page 4 and stop after "right here" on page 8.)

After Reading

Ask the following comprehension questions:

(+ or −)

☐ 1. **What do Beaver and Hedgehog pack for the picnic?** (cloth, cups, plums)

☐ 2. **What do they bring instead of apples?** (plums)

☐ 3. **What is Beaver's plan when it starts to rain?** (They can have the picnic inside the house.)

☐ 4. **Why do they pack a cloth?** (to sit on)

☐ 5. **What does Beaver place on the list?** (checks)

© Harcourt

Individual Reading Inventory

"Here is the cloth," said Hedgehog.	6
"I will check it off my list," said Beaver. *Check*.	16
Beaver put a check beside *cloth*.	22
"The cups can go in the front," said Hedgehog.	31
Check. Beaver put a check beside *cups*.	38
"We don't have any apples," said Beaver.	45
"Here are some plums," said Hedgehog.	51
All the things went in the bag.	58
"Now we are ready!" said Beaver.	64
"I'm sorry, Beaver," said Hedgehog. "I don't	71
think we can go for a picnic. It is raining."	81
Beaver looked out the window. It was raining.	89
"I have a plan," Beaver said.	95
"We don't need to go to the park," said Beaver.	105
"We can have our picnic here."	111

Comments _____

_____

_____

Grade _1_ **Level** _OL_

Reader's Name: _____ Date: _____

Title and Author: _*Duck's Visit* by A.M. Jackson_

Word Count: _110_

Number of Errors: Word Recognition _____ Comprehension _____

Meets Benchmark: Yes _____ No _____

Before Reading

Introduce the book:
In this story, Duck is going to visit Dog. Read to find out what happens when Duck loses her map to Dog's house. Then I will ask you some questions. (Have the child begin on page 6 and stop after "at the bus stop" on page 8).

After Reading

Ask the following comprehension questions:

(+ or −)

☐ 1. **Who is Duck visiting?** (Dog)

☐ 2. **Where does Dog live?** (in the city)

☐ 3. **What happens after Duck gets off the bus?** (She can't find her map.)

☐ 4. **How does Duck feel when she loses her map? Why?** (worried, because she is lost)

☐ 5. **How does Duck feel when she sees Dog?** (better)

Individual Reading Inventory

Duck got off the bus in the city. She reached	10
in her bag for the map, but it was not there.	21
"I must have left my map on the bus," she	31
said to the hippo driving the bus.	38
He looked on the bus. "I'm sorry," he said.	47
"I can't find any map. There is nothing here."	56
Duck sat on a bench. "Oh, dear," she said,	65
"how will I find Dog's place?"	71
She thought about what was on the map.	79
"Do I go down Ivy Street first? Maybe I go	89
down Bone Road."	92
"Hi, Duck."	94
Duck looked up. There was Dog! He had	102
come to meet Duck at the bus stop.	110

Comments _____

_____

_____

Grade _1_ **Level** _AL_

Reader's Name: _____ **Date:** _____

Title and Author: _Raccoon and Otter Make Muffins by A.M. Jackson_

Word Count: _116_

Number of Errors: Word Recognition _____ Comprehension _____

Meets Benchmark: Yes _____ No _____

Before Reading

Introduce the book:
In this story, Raccoon and Otter want to make apple muffins. Read to find out what happens. Then I will ask you some questions. (Have the child begin with "I can't find" on page 6 and stop at "and smiled." on page 8.)

After Reading

Ask the following comprehension questions:

(+ or −)

☐	1. **Who is this story about?** (Raccoon, Otter, and Hippo)
☐	2. **Why can't Raccoon and Otter make apple muffins?** (They don't have any apples.)
☐	3. **What kind of food does Hippo like?** (apples)
☐	4. **Why do Raccoon and Otter look at their feet?** (They don't have food to give Hippo.)
☐	5. **Why do Raccoon and Otter smile?** (Hippo has apples.)

© Harcourt

Individual Reading Inventory

"I can't find any apples," said Raccoon.	7
Otter helped Raccoon look for an apple,	14
but they could not find one.	20
"We can't have apple muffins without	26
any apples!" cried Raccoon.	30
"Now we have nothing at all to give Hippo."	39
Just then, there was a tap at the front	48
door. Raccoon opened the door for Hippo.	55
"Hi, Raccoon! Hi, Otter!" said Hippo. "Do	62
I smell food? I am very hungry."	69
Otter and Raccoon looked down at their feet.	77
"I'm sorry, Hippo," said Otter.	82
"We have nothing to eat."	87
Hippo smiled. "It's lucky I have some	94
apples for us," she said, opening her	101
paper bag. "I really like apples."	107
Otter and Raccoon looked at each other	114
and smiled.	116

Comments _____

_____

_____

_____

© Harcourt

Grade ___2___ Level ___BL___

Reader's Name: _____ Date: _____

Title and Author: _*Apples for Sheep and Goat* by Rachel Johns_

Word Count: ___126___

Number of Errors: Word Recognition _____ Comprehension _____

Meets Benchmark: Yes _____ No _____

Before Reading

Introduce the book:
Read this story to find out how Sheep and Goat get to the apples. Then I will ask you some questions. (Have the child begin on page 6 with "Goat, look" and read to the end of page 12.)

After Reading

Ask the following comprehension questions:

(+ or –)

☐ 1. **How does Goat think they should get to the apples?** (by boat)

☐ 2. **Why do you think it was a bad idea for Sheep and Goat to take the boat?** (They got too tired to row across the river.)

☐ 3. **Who pulls Sheep and Goat's boat out of the river?** (Farmer)

☐ 4. **What do they build over the river?** (a bridge)

☐ 5. **What do you think Sheep, Goat, and Farmer will do after they walk across the bridge?** (Eat the apples.)

© Harcourt

Individual Reading Inventory

"Goat, look at the lovely apples over there,"	8
cried Sheep.	10
Goat could not believe her eyes.	16
Goat saw a boat.	20
"We will row across and get some apples," she said.	30
They got in the boat and began to row.	39
Soon they got tired.	43
Farmer saw Goat and Sheep.	48
He waded out to them and brought the boat back.	58
"I do not understand why you are in a boat," he said.	70
"Your apples across the river look quite tasty,"	78
said Sheep.	80
Farmer saw the apples.	84
"Now I understand," he said.	89
Early the next morning, Farmer came in his truck.	98
"We will build a bridge over the river," he said.	108
Sheep and Goat helped Farmer build the bridge.	116
When the bridge was finished, they all walked	124
across it.	126

Comments _____

_____

_____

_____

© Harcourt

Grade ____2____ Level ____OL____

Reader's Name: _____ **Date:** _____

Title and Author: ____*The Country Show* by Rachel Johns____

Word Count: ____139____

Number of Errors: Word Recognition _____ Comprehension _____

Meets Benchmark: Yes _____ No _____

Before Reading

Introduce the book:
Read this story to find out why Cow, Horse, and Chicken are upset. Then I will ask you some questions. (Have the child begin on page 8 with "The animals went" and read to page 12 at "needed the animals.")

After Reading

Ask the following comprehension questions:

(+ or −)

☐ 1. **What do the animals want from Farmer?** (to be looked after like Goat)

☐ 2. **What reason does Farmer give for not looking after the other animals like Goat?** (He doesn't have the time.)

☐ 3. **Who gives the animals the idea to go on strike?** (Cat)

☐ 4. **Read page 8 again. What do you think *go on strike* means?** (to not do anything for someone until the person does what you want)

☐ 5. **Do you think Farmer will give the animals what they want? Explain your answer.** (Yes, because then he can get what he wants from the animals.)

Individual Reading Inventory

They knocked on Farmer's door. He could not believe 9
the animals all wanted to be looked after like Goat. 19

"That's impossible," he said. "I don't have the time." 28

The animals went back to the barnyard feeling 36
quite sorry for themselves. Cat listened to them 44
complain again. 46

"Why don't you go on strike?" he suggested. 54
"Don't do anything for Farmer until he does 62
what you want." 65

The next day, Farmer went to get the milk from Cow. 76

"No milk?" Farmer exclaimed. 80

"I have no time to make milk," said Cow. 89

Then, Farmer went to ride Horse to the market, but 99
Horse wouldn't move. 102

"No ride today?" he exclaimed. 107

"I have no time to take you there," said Horse. 117

Finally, Farmer went to get eggs from Chicken's 125
nest. 126

"No eggs?" he exclaimed. 130

"I have no time to lay eggs," said Chicken. 139

Comments _____

_____

_____

_____

Grade _2_ **Level** _AL_

Reader's Name: _____ Date: _____

Title and Author: _*Rooster's Sore Throat* by Rachel Johns_

Word Count: _119_

Number of Errors: Word Recognition _____ Comprehension _____

Meets Benchmark: Yes _____ No _____

Before Reading

Introduce the book:

In this story, Rooster cannot crow because he has a sore throat. Read to find out what happens. Then I will ask you some questions. (Have the child begin on page 11 with "The next morning" and read to page 13 to "without you.")

After Reading

Ask the following comprehension questions:

(+ or –)

☐ 1. **Why did Farmer oversleep?** (Rooster didn't crow at sunrise.)

☐ 2. **What do you think Farmer and Rooster talked about?** (that Rooster needed to rest)

☐ 3. **Who did Farmer call to a meeting?** (Cow and Goat)

☐ 4. **If you were Farmer, would you send the animals on vacation? Why or why not?** (Responses will vary.)

☐ 5. **Why do you think Rooster wanted Cow and Goat to go on vacation with him?** (Possible responses: Rooster didn't like being alone; Cow and Goat were Rooster's friends.)

Individual Reading Inventory

The next morning, no one crowed at sunrise.	8
Farmer slept until the middle of the morning.	16
He did not understand how he could have slept	25
so late.	27
Then he remembered that Rooster was sick.	34
"I have had enough of this," Farmer said.	42
He went to see Rooster. They talked for a long time.	53
Then Farmer got in his truck and went to town.	63
When he returned, he called Cow and Goat to a	73
meeting. "I have brought something for you," he said.	82
Farmer gave each animal an envelope.	88
Cow and Goat opened the envelopes.	94
"These are bus tickets to the beach," they cried	103
in amazement. "We don't understand!"	108
"Rooster needs a vacation," said Farmer.	114
"He won't go without you."	119

Comments _____

_____

_____

_____

Grade __2__ Level __BL__

Reader's Name: _____ Date: _____

Title and Author: *Thomas Alva Edison: A Great Inventor* by Jordan Maxwell

Word Count: __142__

Number of Errors: Word Recognition _____ Comprehension _____

Meets Benchmark: Yes _____ No _____

Before Reading

Introduce the book:
Read this story to find out how Thomas Alva Edison became an inventor. Then I will ask you some questions. (Have the child begin on page 4 with "Thomas was born" and end on page 9 at "Menlo Park, New Jersey.")

After Reading

Ask the following comprehension questions:

(+ or –)

☐ 1. **Where was Thomas born?** (in Ohio)

☐ 2. **Why did Thomas's mother start teaching him at home?** (because he was not doing well at school)

☐ 3. **When Thomas was twelve, how did he earn money?** (He sold newspapers on trains.)

☐ 4. **Why do you think it is important for an inventor to like to do experiments?** (Inventors have to try many experiments before they find something that works.)

☐ 5. **Do you think being an inventor would be easy or hard? Explain your answer.** (Responses will vary.)

Individual Reading Inventory

Thomas was born in Ohio in 1847.	7
When he was seven years old, he and his family	17
moved to Port Huron, Michigan.	22
They lived on a farm there.	28
Thomas did not do well in school.	35
When he was eight, his mother began to	43
teach him at home.	47
Thomas liked learning, and he liked	53
to do experiments.	56
Thomas began to earn money when he	63
was twelve. He got supplies of newspapers,	70
and he sold them on trains.	76
When he was sixteen, Thomas got a job	84
working a telegraph machine. The telegraph	90
sent messages through telephone wires.	95
Thomas didn't want to work on the telegraph	103
forever. He wanted a career as an inventor.	111

Individual Reading Inventory

In 1875, Thomas moved into his own 118
workshop in New Jersey. There he worked 125
as an inventor. 128

The next year, Thomas moved into a new 136
workshop in Menlo Park, New Jersey. 142

Comments _____

_____

_____

_____

Grade _2_ **Level** _OL_

Reader's Name: _____ **Date:** _____

Title and Author: *Madame C. J. Walker: Making Dreams Happen*

by Jordan Maxwell

Word Count: _149_

Number of Errors: Word Recognition _____ Comprehension _____

Meets Benchmark: Yes _____ No _____

Before Reading

Introduce the book:

This story is about Madame C.J. Walker and how she started her business. Read to find out about her life. Then I will ask you some questions. (Have the child begin on page 9 with "Sarah moved" and read to page 13, stopping at "earn money, too.")

After Reading

Ask the following comprehension questions:

(+ or −)

☐ 1. **After Sarah left her job as a cook, what did she sell?** (hair product)

☐ 2. **How did Sarah get the name Madam C.J. Walker?** (She married a man named C.J. Walker.)

☐ 3. **Why do you think she didn't sell her product in a store?** (She could move around the country and sell her product to more people.)

☐ 4. **How do you know Madam Walker's business grew?** (She built a factory; she had a lot of women selling her product)

☐ 5. **Why do you think people admire Madam C.J. Walker?** (because she was successful and helped others)

Individual Reading Inventory

Sarah moved to Denver where she worked as   8
a cook and saved her money. Before long, she   17
was able to leave her job and start selling   26
her new hair product.   30

Sarah then married a man named C.J. Walker. She   39
decided to call herself Madam C.J. Walker, and she   48
used the name for her products.   54

Madam Walker sold her products door to door and   63
through mail order. She moved around the country,   71
talking about her work. She also trained African   79
American women to help sell her products.   86

In 1910, Madam Walker moved to Indianapolis. She   94
built a factory and another training school there.   102
She soon had five thousand women selling   109
her products throughout the country.   114

⇨

 © Harcourt

Individual Reading Inventory

Madam Walker became one of the most   121

successful women of her day. Not only was she   130

wealthy, but she was able to provide   137

hundreds of African American women   142

with a way to earn money, too.   149

Comments _____

_____

_____

_____

Grade ___2___ **Level** ___AL___

Reader's Name: _____ **Date:** _____

Title and Author: *Cyrus McCormick: Friend to Farmers* by Jordan Maxwell

Word Count: ___143___

Number of Errors: Word Recognition _____ Comprehension _____

Meets Benchmark: Yes _____ No _____

Before Reading

Introduce the book:
Read this story to learn about Cyrus McCormick and the reaper he invented. Then I will ask you some questions. (Have the child begin on page 6 with "Harvesting was" and read to the end of page 10.)

After Reading

Ask the following comprehension questions:

(+ or −)

1. **What is a reaper?** (a machine that cuts grain crops)

2. **If you had been with the farmers when Cyrus showed them his strange looking reaper, would you have believed him? Explain your answer.**
   (Responses will vary.)

3. **What is one way that Cyrus improved his reaper?**
   (He added a blade that cut grain in wet weather.)

4. **Whose reaper won in the challenge on the day it rained?** (Cyrus's)

5. **Why do you think Cyrus sold twenty-nine reapers in 1843?** (He proved to farmers that it worked.)

Individual Reading Inventory

Harvesting was very difficult.	4
In 1831, Cyrus made a reaper that did	12
cut grain crops. The reaper also removed	19
the hard outer shells of the grain.	26
Cyrus's machine could cut the grain crop	33
much faster than a person.	38
Farmers came to see Cyrus's reaper,	44
but they didn't believe it would work.	51
They thought it looked like a wheelbarrow,	58
a carriage, and a flying machine!	64
The farmers returned home and	69
kept using their old tools.	74
Cyrus did not give up. For the next ten years,	84
he did experiments to improve his reaper.	91
He added a blade that cut grain in wet weather.	101

Individual Reading Inventory

In 1843, an inventor of another reaper	108
challenged Cyrus to see whose machine would	115
cut more grain. Luckily, it rained on the day of	125
the contest. The other reaper jammed up,	132
but Cyrus's machine kept working.	137
That year, Cyrus sold twenty-nine reapers.	143

Comments _____

_____

_____

_____

Grade 2 **Level** BL

Before Reading

Introduce the book:
In this story, Abalone wishes to be brightly colored. Read to find out if the Sea grants his wish. Then I will ask you some questions. (Have the child begin on page 5 with "I gave you" and read to the end of page 11 at "Very well.")

After Reading

Ask the following comprehension questions:

(+ or –)

☐ 1. **Why did the Sea give Abalone a gray shell?** (to hide him from his enemies)

☐ 2. **Why is Abalone sad?** (He wants to be colorful.)

☐ 3. **If you were Abalone, would you be happy being gray? Why or why not.** (Responses will vary.)

☐ 4. **Why do people try to catch the rainbow fish?** (because he is so easy to see)

☐ 5. **What do you think the Sea will do? Why?** (Possible response: Change Abalone's color to teach him a lesson.)

Individual Reading Inventory

"I gave you a gray shell to hide you 9
from your enemies," said the sea. 15
"You are never preyed upon because 21
you are never noticed. Surely that 27
must please you." 30

Abalone was still weighed down 35
with sadness. A bright blue crab was 42
scampering past him. 45

"Look at Crab," he cried. 50
"See how beautiful *she* is." 55

"Crab is never safe," the Sea said. 62
"Big fish see her from a long way off, 71
and they make her their dinner. 77
I have made you gray, and I will not 86
budge from my decision." 90

"Look at the beautiful rainbow fish," 96
said Abalone. "He is the most majestic 103
fish in the ocean." 107

⇨

Individual Reading Inventory

"Yes, but people are always trying to   114
catch him because he is so easy to see,"   123
said the Sea.   126

    Abalone listened but did not hear.   132
All he wanted was to be bright and   140
beautiful.   141

    Day after day, he asked and asked   148
until, at last, the Sea gave in.   155

    "Very well," said the Sea.   160

Comments _____

_____

_____

_____

Grade ___2___ **Level** ___OL___

Reader's Name: _____ **Date:** _____

Title and Author: *How Tortoise Got Its Shell* by Jake Harris

Word Count: ___161___

Number of Errors: Word Recognition _____ Comprehension _____

Meets Benchmark: Yes _____ No _____

Before Reading

Introduce the book:
Read this story to find out how Tortoise got his shell. Then I will ask you some questions. (Have the child begin on page 3 with "Long ago," and read to the end of page 7.)

After Reading

Ask the following comprehension questions:

(+ or −)

☐ 1. **Which animal did Forest forget to give a home to?** (Tortoise)

☐ 2. **Why would Lizard lie on the rocks?** (to be in the warm sun)

☐ 3. **Which character in the story would you like to be? Why?** (Responses will vary.)

☐ 4. **Why was Tortoise unhappy?** (Forest had not given him a home.)

☐ 5. **What do you think Forest will do when he remembers Tortoise has no home? Why?** (He will give Tortoise a home, because I know that it has its shell as a home.)

Individual Reading Inventory

Long ago, Forest gave each animal	6
its own home—each animal, that is,	13
except for Tortoise. He was forgotten.	19
Lizard was given a home between	25
the rocks. On hot days, Lizard could be	33
seen scampering up on the rocks to lie	41
in the warm sun.	45
Crab's home was in a hole in the sand,	54
under a coconut palm. The hole was	61
cool and dark inside. It was the perfect	69
home for Crab.	72
Snake was given a home beneath the	79
fallen leaves of the forest. The leaves	86
sheltered him from storms and hid him	93
from other animals.	96
Owl's home was a hole in a majestic,	104
old tree. The hole was dark and cozy.	112
It kept Owl hidden until night when he	120
would come out to hunt.	125

Individual Reading Inventory

The animals thanked Forest for their   131
homes. They were all happy, except for   138
Tortoise.   139

   One night, a terrible storm came.   145
The rain fell heavily, and Tortoise   151
needed to find a home to stay warm   159
and dry.   161

Comments _____

_____

_____

_____

Reader's Name: _____ Date: _____

Title and Author: ___*Why Tree Frog Sings at Night* by Jake Harris___

Word Count: ___167___

Number of Errors: Word Recognition _____ Comprehension _____

Meets Benchmark: Yes _____ No _____

Before Reading

Introduce the book:
Read this story to find out why Tree Frog sings at night. Then I will ask you some questions. (Have the child begin on page 9 with "Tree Frog's songs" and read to the end of page 12.)

After Reading

Ask the following comprehension questions:

(+ or −)

☐ 1. **What do the animals mean when they say Tree Frog's songs aren't fit for anyone to hear?** (Tree Frog is a bad singer.)

☐ 2. **Who tells Tree Frog they don't like his singing?** (Duck)

☐ 3. **Who discovers Tree Frog when he is crying?** (Moon)

☐ 4. **Do you think it was a good solution for Tree Frog to sing at night instead of during the day? Explain your answer.** (Possible response: Yes, because Tree Frog can keep Moon company without bothering the other animals.)

☐ 5. **What reason does Moon give for wanting Tree Frog to sing at night?** (Moon gets lonely at night.)

Individual Reading Inventory

"Tree Frog's songs aren't fit for *anyone* to hear,"   9
the pond animals said to one another.   16
"It is a great pity, but one of us will have to   28
tell him the truth."   32

"Then the task is up to me," said Duck calmly.   42

When Tree Frog heard what Duck had to say,   51
he burst into tears. He was weighed down   59
with such sadness that he cried pitifully   66
all day and into the night.   72

It was Moon who later made the sad   80
discovery of poor Tree Frog sobbing.   86
Moon took pity on him. "What is the matter,   95
Tree Frog?" Moon asked kindly.   100

Tree Frog peered up at Moon.   106
"The pond animals do not enjoy my   113
singing during the day," he wept.   119
"They want me to stop,"   124

Moon was filled with pity.   129

Individual Reading Inventory

"Why," said Moon, "if the pond animals   136

do not like your singing during the day,   144

then you must sing for me at night.   152

I am often lonely in the darkest hours,   160

and your voice will keep me company."   167

Comments _____

_____

_____

_____

Grade _____3_____ Level _____BL_____

Reader's Name: _____ Date: _____

Title and Author: _____*How Bear Lost His Tail* adapted by Martin Curtis_____

Word Count: _____151_____

Number of Errors: Word Recognition _____ Comprehension _____

Meets Benchmark: Yes _____ No _____

Before Reading

Introduce the book:

Read this story to find out why Coyote wants to teach Bear a lesson. Then I will ask you some questions. (Have the student begin on page 5 with "Everyone was tired" and stop after "'I can teach you,' said Coyote." on page 8.)

After Reading

Ask the following comprehension questions:

(+ or −)

☐ 1. **What was everyone tired of?** (Bear bragging about his tail)

☐ 2. **Where does Coyote go after he compliments Bear's tail?** (to the pond)

☐ 3. **How can you tell Coyote is going to play a trick on Bear?** (He isn't really fishing with his tail, but he wants Bear to think he is.)

☐ 4. **Reread page 7. What do you think it means that Bear *felt as hungry as if he were living through a famine?*** (that he is very hungry)

☐ 5. **Do you think Bear will accept Coyote's offers to teach him to fish with his tail? Why or why not?** (Yes, because Bear is hungry and wants to catch lots of fish.)

© Harcourt

Individual Reading Inventory

Everyone was tired of Bear's bragging,	6
especially Coyote. He decided it was	12
time to teach Bear a lesson.	18
"Your tail is beautiful!" exclaimed Coyote.	24
"The fur is thick and shiny. See you later!"	33
Then Coyote ran to the pond.	39
The pond was covered in ice.	45
Coyote found a place where he knew Bear	53
would see him. He broke a hole in the ice	63
and began to catch fish. He piled the fish	72
around the hole. When he saw Bear,	79
Coyote dropped his tail into the hole in the ice.	89
Bear saw Coyote and the piles of fish.	97
He felt as hungry as if he were living through	107
a famine. Then he saw that Coyote's tail was	116
hanging in the water. Bear's gaze was filled	124
with curiosity.	126
"What are you doing?" asked Bear.	132
"I'm fishing," replied Coyote.	136
"I've never seen anyone fish like that," said Bear.	145
"I can teach you," said Coyote.	151

Comments _____

_____

_____

_____

© Harcourt

Grade _____3_____   Level _____OL_____

Reader's Name: _____ Date: _____

Title and Author: *The Coat of Patches, A Yiddish Folktale* adapted by Cynthia Burres

Word Count: _____157_____

Number of Errors: Word Recognition _____ Comprehension _____

Meets Benchmark: Yes _____ No _____

Before Reading

Introduce the book:

In this story, Khaim goes out to earn money for his family. Read to find out what he does with the money he earns. Then I will ask you some questions. (Have the student begin on page 5 with "Khaim set out" and read to the end of page 6.)

After Reading

Ask the following comprehension questions:

(+ or −)

☐ 1. **What does Khaim do in the story?** (First he sets out. Next he asks for work to do. Then he digs a well. Next he changed his coins to paper money. Finally, he sews his money into his coat under patches.)

☐ 2. **What is the first job Khaim is hired to do?** (dig a well)

☐ 3. **How did the man pay Khaim for digging the well?** (generously with silver coins)

☐ 4. **If you were a villager in the story, what work would you hire Khaim to do for you?** (Responses will vary.)

☐ 5. **What are some other things Khaim could have done with his money to keep it safe?** (Possible responses: put it in a bank, hid it, given it to his family)

© Harcourt

Individual Reading Inventory

Khaim set out the next morning, taking nothing	8
but the coat he wore. He walked and walked for	18
many miles until he reached another village.	25
Khaim went to every house, and he asked whether	34
there was any work for him. There was none.	43
Finally, when he reached the last house,	50
he knocked on the door and a man answered.	59
"Excuse me, sir," Khaim said. "I need work.	67
Is there anything you need?"	72
"Can you dig a well?" replied the man.	80
"Absolutely!" said Khaim confidently.	84
Khaim worked all day, and when he finished,	92
the man was extremely generous.	97
He paid Khaim with silver coins.	103
Khaim knew he had to be careful because he	112
could lose the money or be robbed. Suddenly,	120
he had a fantastic idea.	125
Khaim hurried into town, changed his coins into	133
paper money, and placed the money inside his coat.	142
Then he sewed a patch over it so that no one could	154
see the money.	157

Comments _____

_____

_____

_____

© Harcourt

Grade ___3___ Level ___AL___

Reader's Name: _____ Date: _____

Title and Author: *The Stonecutter* by author Damon Johnson _____

Word Count: ___157___

Number of Errors: Word Recognition _____ Comprehension _____

Meets Benchmark: Yes _____ No _____

Before Reading

Introduce the book:

In this story, Hiroshi wishes he had a bigger home. Read to find out if his wish is granted. Then I will ask you some questions. (Have the student begin on page 7 with "Suddenly the mountain" and stop at page 8 after "must be a rich man!")

After Reading

Ask the following comprehension questions:

(+ or –)

☐ 1. **Why do you think Hiroshi felt suspicious?** (He did not know where the voice was coming from.)

☐ 2. **What was Hiroshi's amazing discovery?** (An enormous palace had replaced his small shack.)

☐ 3. **How did Hiroshi realize he was in the right place?** (He recognized some trees.)

☐ 4. **If you were Hiroshi, would you believe your shack had changed to a palace? Explain your answer.** (Responses will vary.)

☐ 5. **What wish did the deep, rumbling voice grant?** (Hiroshi's wish for a rich man's house.)

© Harcourt

Individual Reading Inventory

Suddenly, the mountain seemed to shake,   6

and Hiroshi heard a deep, rumbling voice   13

that boomed, "Your wish is granted!"   19

Hiroshi looked around and instantly felt   25

suspicious. Was someone trying to play a   32

trick on him?   35

Hiroshi trudged home slowly that night   41

because he did not want to return to his   50

small shack. However, the shack was Hiroshi's   57

home, and it was the only place he knew.   66

When Hiroshi came to the foot of the mountain,   75

he made an amazing discovery. His shack had   83

vanished, and there was an enormous palace   90

in its place.   93

"I must have come down the wrong side of   102

the mountain!" Hiroshi thought. "I simply wasn't   109

paying any attention." Then he recognized some   116

trees, and he realized he was in the right place.   126

"It is true!" he thought with astonishment.   133

"The mountain is so generous! It has given me a   143

rich man's house. Now, I too, must be a rich man!"   154

Comments _____

_____

_____

_____

© Harcourt

Grade ____3____ Level ____BL____

Reader's Name: _____ Date: _____

Title and Author: ____*Favorite Fables* retold by Emily Kavicky____

Word Count: ____171____

Number of Errors: Word Recognition _____ Comprehension _____

Meets Benchmark: Yes _____ No _____

Before Reading

Introduce the book:

Read this story to find out how the lion and the mouse become friends. Then I will ask you some questions. (Have the student read pages 4 through 6.)

After Reading

Ask the following comprehension questions:

(+ or −)

☐ 1. **Why didn't the lion eat the mouse?** (He decided the mouse wasn't a big enough meal.)

☐ 2. **How does the mouse help the lion?** (He chews through the ropes to free the lion.)

☐ 3. **After he frees the lion, why do you think the mouse is afraid?** (He thinks the lion is going to eat him.)

☐ 4. **What lesson does the story give at the end?** (that it doesn't matter how big friends are but rather how good of friends they are)

☐ 5. **What is another lesson you can learn from the story?** (Possible response: Be nice to others and they will be nice to you.)

© Harcourt

Individual Reading Inventory

"I am going to eat you, little mouse,"   8

exclaimed the lion.   11

"Oh, please don't eat me,"   16

begged the little mouse.   20

The lion decided that the mouse wasn't big   28

enough to make a good meal. He let the mouse go.   39

A few days later, the little mouse   46

overheard a great roar and discovered   52

the lion caught in some ropes.   58

"I have been caught by a hunter.   65

Please help me!" cried the lion.   71

The little mouse said, "You set me free,   79

so I will help you." The little mouse jumped   88

on top of the lion and chewed apart the ropes.   98

The ropes fell away, and the lion was free.   107

The lion shook off the ropes and grabbed   115

the little mouse. For a moment, the mouse   123

was afraid, but the grateful lion hugged the   131

mouse in his big paws.   136

From that day on, the lion and the mouse   145

were best friends. The lion learned that it does   154

not matter how big or small your friends are.   163

It matters how good a friend they are!   171

Comments _____

_____

_____

_____

© Harcourt

Grade ___3___ Level ___OL___

Reader's Name: _____ Date: _____

Title and Author: *Coyote and Rabbit, A Tale from the Southwest* by Ron Lewis

Word Count: ___154___

Number of Errors: Word Recognition _____ Comprehension _____

Meets Benchmark: Yes _____ No _____

Before Reading

Introduce the book:

In this story, Coyote wants Rabbit to teach him his tricks. Read to find out what Rabbit shows Coyote. Then I will ask you some questions. (Have the student begin on page 10 with "Rabbit showed" and read to the end of page 11.)

After Reading

Ask the following comprehension questions:

(+ or −)

☐ 1. **What is the first trick of Rabbit's that Coyote already knows?** (how Rabbit hides in the brush)

☐ 2. **What happens when Rabbit stops quickly?** (Coyote runs right past him.)

☐ 3. **Why can't Coyote do the quick step to the side?** (Coyote's eyes are in the wrong place.)

☐ 4. **How are your eyes more like Coyote's eyes than Rabbit's eyes?** (Like Coyote's eyes, mine are in the front of my head.)

☐ 5. **Do you think Rabbit is a good teacher? Explain your answer.** (Responses will vary.)

© Harcourt

Individual Reading Inventory

Rabbit showed Coyote how he could hide	7
in the brush, but Coyote already knew this.	15
Rabbit showed Coyote how he often ran in circles,	24
but Coyote knew this, too. Rabbit showed him	32
how he stopped so quickly that Coyote would	40
just run right past him.	45
"I have seen these things many times,	52
so show me a trick I don't know," demanded Coyote.	62
"My best trick is a quick step to the side,"	72
said Rabbit. "Try it."	76
Coyote tried it several times,	81
but could not do it like Rabbit.	88
"I think the problem is that your eyes	96
are in the wrong place," declared Rabbit.	103
"There's absolutely nothing wrong with	108
my eyes," said Coyote.	112
"Not for a Coyote, perhaps," said Rabbit.	119
"I am a rabbit, so my eyes are on the sides	130
of my head, and I see well to the side.	140
Your eyes are in the front of your head,	149
so you cannot see to the side."	154

Comments _____

_____

_____

_____

© Harcourt

Grade ____3____ Level ____AL____

Reader's Name: _____ **Date:** _____

Title and Author: _*Groundhog's New Home*_ by author Keith Yoder _____

Word Count: ____169____

Number of Errors: Word Recognition _____ Comprehension _____

Meets Benchmark: Yes _____ No _____

Before Reading

Introduce the book:

Read this story to find out why Groundhog must find a new home. Then I will ask you some questions. (Have the student begin at the middle of page 3 with "Days were" and stop at the top of page 5 at "to avoid trouble.")

After Reading

Ask the following comprehension questions:

(+ or −)

☐ 1. **List some of the reasons the barn is a good place for Groundhog's burrow.** (It is protected from the wind, dry, cozy, and safe.)

☐ 2. **How can you tell that the man is going to start farming?** (He unloads a tractor and farming supplies.)

☐ 3. **What does Groundhog mean when he says that there will be problems for him?** (The man won't let him live in the barn, and the dog will hunt him.)

☐ 4. **How does Groundhog feel about having to move?** (He is sad.)

☐ 5. **If you were Groundhog, would you stay in your burrow in the barn or move? Explain your answer.** (Responses will vary.)

© Harcourt

Individual Reading Inventory

Days were quiet now because the farmer	7
had grown older and no longer farmed.	14
Groundhog had dug his burrow in the barn	22
for protection from the wind, and it remained	30
dry and cozy in winter. He had built many	39
tunnels under the barn and had a good, safe home.	49
Something was changing, though. A man had	56
driven up the lane, gotten out of his truck, and	66
unloaded a small tractor and other farming supplies.	74
From the back of his truck jumped an enormous dog.	84
Groundhog retreated underground and heard the	90
dog sniffing at the end of his burrow.	98
As the man returned to his truck, Groundhog	106
realized what this meant. "There will be life	114
again on this farm, but where there are farmers	123
and dogs, there will be problems for me.	131
I will have to move," he thought sadly.	139
Groundhog wouldn't have to move far, though.	146
He knew of a perfect place up the hill,	155
along a ridge. It was just far enough away for	165
him to avoid trouble.	169

Comments _____

_____

_____

_____

© Harcourt

Grade _____3_____ Level _____BL_____

Reader's Name: _____ **Date:** _____

Title and Author: _____*Earth's Moon* by Kitt Winston_____

Word Count: ____169____

Number of Errors: Word Recognition _____ Comprehension _____

Meets Benchmark: Yes _____ No _____

Before Reading

Introduce the book:

Read this story to learn about the moon. Then I will ask you some questions. (Have the student read pages 11 through 14.)

After Reading

Ask the following comprehension questions:

(+ or −)

☐ 1. **What did the first spacecrafts do?** (They orbited the moon.)

☐ 2. **What was special about the spacecraft that landed on the moon on July 20, 1969?** (It was carrying astronauts.)

☐ 3. **How do you think people felt watching the moon landing on television?** (Possible response: amazed, excited)

☐ 4. **What do scientists do with the moon rocks brought back by astronauts?** (The scientists study the rocks to see how the moon might have formed.)

☐ 5. **Do you think the scientists are right that the moon used to be part of Earth? Explain your answer.** (Responses will vary.)

Individual Reading Inventory

Starting in the 1950s, spacecraft were sent	7
to study the moon. The spacecraft orbited	14
the moon. In this way, scientists learned more	22
and more about the moon.	27
Then, on July 20, 1969, the first spacecraft	35
carrying astronauts from the earth actually	41
landed on the moon! People were able to	49
watch as a person walked on the moon's	57
surface for the first time ever. It was on	66
television!	67
The astronauts sent the pictures of the moon	75
back to the earth. The astronauts brought moon	83
rocks back to the earth. From the rocks, scientists	92
have learned a lot about the moon. The rocks	101
were evidence that the scientists could study to	109
find out how the moon might have been formed.	118
Scientists think the moon might once have	125
been part of the earth. They think a large object	135
from space hit the earth millions of years ago.	144
The dust and ashes from the earth went into space	154
and formed the moon. People have learned a lot	163
about the moon since early times!	169

Comments _____

_____

_____

_____

Grade _____3_____ Level _____OL_____

Reader's Name: _____ **Date:** _____

Title and Author: _*Star Patterns in the Sky* by author Dixie Marshall_

Word Count: _____178_____

Number of Errors: Word Recognition _____ Comprehension _____

Meets Benchmark: Yes _____ No _____

Before Reading

Introduce the book:

Read this story to learn about stars. Then I will ask you some questions. (Have the student begin on page 3 with "People have always" and stop on page 5 after "move in a circle.")

After Reading

Ask the following comprehension questions:

(+ or −)

☐ 1. **What causes stars to light up in the sky?** (the burning gases)

☐ 2. **Which is the closest star to our planet?** (the sun)

☐ 3. **What are some facts you have learned about stars.** (Stars are huge balls of burning gases; stars have a fixed position in space; stars look like they move across the sky.)

☐ 4. **Reread page 4. What does it mean when Earth rotates?** (Earth spins on its axis.)

☐ 5. **Where on Earth would it look like stars are moving in a circle?** (at the North and South Poles)

Individual Reading Inventory

People have always enjoyed watching the stars	7
in the night sky. On a clear night, you might see	18
thousands of stars. A star is really a huge ball of	29
burning gases. It is the burning gases that	37
cause the stars to light up in the sky.	46
The sun is also a star. Its light reflects off	56
the surface of the earth. It is the closest star	66
to our planet.	69
Early in the evening, faraway stars appear	76
over the horizon. As the night goes on, the stars	86
seem to move across the sky from east to west.	96
It is not the stars that move, but the earth.	106
The stars have a fixed position in space.	114
That is, they do not move like the earth or	124
the moon. Earth rotates, or spins on its axis.	133
As the earth turns, the pattern of stars	141
marches across the sky.	145
Stars that are over the center of Earth	153
look like they move in a straight line across	162
the sky. At the North and South Poles,	170
stars look like they move in a circle.	178

Comments _____

_____

_____

_____

Grade ___3___ Level ___AL___

Reader's Name: _____ Date: _____

Title and Author: _*The Sun and the Stars* by Scarlett Jones_

Word Count: ___173___

Number of Errors: Word Recognition _____ Comprehension _____

Meets Benchmark: Yes _____ No _____

Before Reading

Introduce the book:

Read this story to learn about the sun and other stars. Then I will ask you some questions. (Have the student begin at the top of page 11 and stop at the middle of page 12 after "bulge in the middle.")

After Reading

Ask the following comprehension questions:

(+ or −)

☐ 1. **Reread page 11. What does it mean that stars go through a life cycle?** (They grow and eventually die.)

☐ 2. **What is a white dwarf star?** (a very small and very old star)

☐ 3. **What are large groups of stars called?** (galaxies)

☐ 4. **What is the name of the galaxy Earth is part of?** (The Milky Way)

☐ 5. **Think about how old you are and then think about how old stars are. How does this make you feel?** (Responses will vary.)

Individual Reading Inventory

The sun is approximately five billion years old.	8
Some stars are older than the sun, and some	17
stars are younger. Stars go through life cycles	25
just like plants and animals do. Super giant	33
stars are very old. As a super giant star	42
burns up its gases, it becomes larger and larger.	51
Eventually it explodes and shrinks to become	58
a very small star called a white dwarf.	66
White dwarf stars are among the oldest stars in space.	76
Small- and medium-size stars, like our sun,	84
will one day become white dwarf stars, too.	92
Of course, this will not happen for another	100
five billion years!	103
There are trillions of stars in space.	110
Most stars are found in large groups called galaxies.	119
One galaxy can have billions of stars in it.	128
Galaxies are also made up of gases and dust,	137
and they come in different sizes and shapes.	145
The earth and our sun are in a galaxy called	155
the Milky Way. The Milky Way is shaped like	164
a spiral with a large bulge in the middle.	173

Comments _____

_____

_____

_____

Grade _____3_____ Level _____OL_____

Reader's Name: _____ **Date:** _____

Title and Author: _____*In the Land of Dinosaurs* by Daphne Greaves_____

Word Count: ____183____

Number of Errors: Word Recognition _____ Comprehension _____

Meets Benchmark: Yes _____ No _____

Before Reading

Introduce the book:

In this story, a group of scientists and students use a time machine to travel back in time. Read to find out what they see. Then I will ask you some questions. (Have the student begin on page 11 with "Dr. Hill: I think" and stop on page 13 after "to confirm that.")

After Reading

Ask the following comprehension questions:

(+ or –)

☐ 1. **What does T. rex look like?** (It is large and tall with huge legs and tiny arms.)

☐ 2. **How long was the team in the past?** (three hours)

☐ 3. **What is Team Rex trying to find out about the T. rex?** (if T. rex is a hunter or a scavenger)

☐ 4. **Why does Team Rex move slowly while approaching T. rex?** (They don't want T. rex to see them.)

☐ 5. **Why is Daniel glad to leave the past?** (A T. rex may have hurt them if they stayed in the past.)

© Harcourt

Individual Reading Inventory

Dr. Hill: I think we may have found T. rex.   10

Everyone move slowly and be steady. Keep low.   18

Narrator 2: The team moved slowly out from   26

behind the trees, and there was T. rex not far away!   37

Narrator 1: The giant dinosaur stood tall on huge   46

legs with its tiny arms waving wildly in the air.   56

Narrator 2: T. rex bellowed loudly. He was obviously   65

angry and headed straight toward Team Rex!   72

Daniel: Look behind us! It's another T. rex.   80

Narrator 1: Two very angry dinosaurs were   87

headed straight toward each other!   92

Narrator 2: Unfortunately, Team Rex was right in the middle!   102

Dr. Reed: Everybody stick together!   107

Narrator 1: Suddenly, the air began to hum, and   116

the group felt themselves spiraling forward in time.   124

Narrator 2: Fortunately, the three hours were up,   132

and Team Rex was headed back to the year 3800!   142

Emma: The only problem is that we didn't get to   152

find out whether T. rex was a hunter or a scavenger.   163

Daniel: I'm not sure I am exactly disappointed   171

about that!   173

Dr. Hill: It will take other trips to confirm that.   183

Comments _____

_____

_____

_____

Grade _____3_____ Level _____AL_____

© Harcourt

Reader's Name: _____ **Date:** _____

Title and Author: _____*Busy Bees and the* Buzz 12 by Daphne Greaves_____

Word Count: _____174_____

Number of Errors: Word Recognition _____ Comprehension _____

Meets Benchmark: Yes _____ No _____

Before Reading

Introduce the book:

In this story, a group of scientists and students ride inside a small machine called the *Buzz 12*. Read to find out what they learn about bees. Then I will ask you some questions. (Have the student begin on page 12 with "Cal: How do" and stop on page 14 after "in the *Buzz 12*."

After Reading

Ask the following comprehension questions:

(+ or –)

☐ 1. **How do the students and scientists travel inside the hive?** (in a small machine called *Buzz 12*)

☐ 2. **What is a honey stomach?** (a pouch inside a honey bee's body with a special substance that turns nectar into honey)

☐ 3. **What do bees eat during the winter?** (honey)

☐ 4. **Why do bees store honey for winter?** (It will be too cold to find food outside.)

☐ 5. **What does Cal think of a bee's life?** (They are lucky they get to eat honey.)

Individual Reading Inventory

Cal: How do the bees turn the nectar into honey?	10
Dr. Silva: They begin by storing it in a special	20
pouch in their bodies called a honey stomach.	28
Dr. Marx: Inside the honey stomach is a special	37
substance. This substance begins the job of	44
turning the nectar into honey.	49
Ashley: What happens next?	53
Dr. Silva: Let's go back to the hive and see.	63
Kiko: *Day Two—When we got back to the hive, we*	74
saw bees putting the mixture from their honey	82
stomachs into special honeycomb cells. Dr. Silva	89
and Dr. Marx explained what happens next.	96
Dr. Marx: The bees remove extra water from	104
the fluid, and it slowly becomes honey. After the	113
honey is made, the worker bees place a	121
beeswax cap over each honeycomb.	126
Dr. Silva: During the winter, the bees will eat the honey.	137
Cal: What a great way to spend the winter. I love	148
honey so much that I could eat it until I erupt!	159
Narrator 1: The group enjoyed a good laugh and	168
flew off in the *Buzz 12.*	174

Comments _____

_____

_____

_____

© Harcourt